CONTENTS

Ships in Focus Publications

Correspondence and editorial:
Roy Fenton
18 Durrington Avenue
London SW20 8NT
020 8879 3527
rfenton@rfenton.demon.co.uk
Orders and photographic:
John & Marion Clarkson
18 Franklands, Longton
Preston PR4 5PD
0845 0760078
shipsinfocus@btinternet.com
© 2007 Individual contributors,
John Clarkson and Roy Fenton.

Printed by Amadeus Press Ltd., Cleckheaton,
Yorkshire.
Designed by Hugh Smallwood, John Clarkson
and Roy Fenton.

SHIPS IN FOCUS RECORD
ISBN 1 901703 82 7

SUBSCRIPTION RATES FOR RECORD

Readers can start their subscription with any
issue, and are welcome to backdate it to
receive previous issues.

	3 issues	4 issues
UK	£24	£31
Europe (airmail)	£26	£34
Rest of the world (surface mail)	£26	£34
Rest of the world (airmail)	£31	£41

SHIPS IN FOCUS RECORD

March

The decision to include book reviews [...]
welcomed. However, the letter we ex[...]
materialised, so perhaps we are being [...]
running reviews, and repeat our requ[...] ...information about,
books that deserve commenting on and for offers of reviews from readers.

As the notional end of a volume, this issue has been extended by our
customary eight pages to provide room for an index, and also includes our usual
colour section, now expanded to 16 pages. We also intend to include some
colour in our next edition, due in July, which has much to do with a waterway
which greatly influenced the development of your editors' appreciation of ships,
the Manchester Ship Canal.

The flow of excellent contributions to 'Record' continues, and in waiting
we have material on shipbreaking in Scotland, the Nigerian cement phenomena,
and an important motor passenger ship rejected by an ailing British company
which had an illustrious career in Australia, and more. This will keep our pages
filled in 2007, but we are always looking at least three issues ahead, so please
keep the contributions coming. We repeat our offer to new contributors to give
reasonable help with research to complete an article, but strongly suggest that
they contact us at an early stage.

Our latest publication, 'Clan Line: Illustrated Fleet History', is
progressing very well and is on track to be published in the late spring. The
minutes of The Clan Line Steamers Ltd. – all 12 volumes of them – have proved
an invaluable source of information on why various decisions were taken and
why ships were built, acquired or disposed of. We believe the book will provide
much previously unpublished material, plus a comprehensive set of photographs
of the attractive and important fleet of cargo ships which belonged to the company
and to the closely associated Houston and Scottish Shire Lines.

This is an appropriate point to mention our policy on publications, as
in recent months we have received a number of proposals from aspiring authors,
most of which we have had to turn down. As with any publisher, our output is
limited by what we can produce and what we can sell. Production involves
editing, laying out, illustrating and proofing – all of which takes time which is at
a premium. Selling involves persuading customers and the declining band of
booksellers to take our books. We therefore tend to publish only books which
we consider from past experience will appeal to our, admittedly rather limited,
market. We are always pleased to consider submissions, but would strongly
suggest that to avoid disappointment anyone approaching us should look very
carefully at our output and consider how well their work fits into it.
John Clarkson.

Roy Fenton

An impressive view of the *Lokoja Palm* in the English Channel. Having no
deck cargo the twin hatches can be clearly seen. *See page 200. [Fotoflite]*

THE FINAL YEARS OF PALM LINE
John Goble

Continuing the story of Palm Line's ships begun in 'Record 35', this article describes the last years before Palm Line became just another item in this country's maritime memory.

When I joined Palm Line at the end of 1976 the British Merchant Navy was at its largest size ever in terms of tonnage flying the Red Ensign. It was far from a similar peak, of course, in the number of ships and hence in the employment offered but it was still healthy enough to be attracting many former seafarers back to sea to enjoy the recently improved salaries. Not enough returnees, however, to prevent T. and J. Harrison making the headlines in the local papers at the time with two ships loaded and prevented from sailing out of Birkenhead for want of junior officers. Yet, only a decade later, Palm Line was gone, just a small part of the catastrophic reduction in the British merchant fleet. Looking back now from the vantage point of a further two decades, how and why did that decline happen and how inevitable was its extinction?

Palm Line was always regarded as one of the lesser lights of the Merchant Navy during its 37 years of existence. For instance, those invaluable and authoritative shipping guides, the Ian Allan 'ABC' pocketbooks, always relegated the fleet for some reason to the 'Ocean Freighters' category. There was a small volume printed privately in 1970 to celebrate the 'coming of age' of Palm from its 1949 origins but the only other printed record of its existence is the 1994 title by Laurence Dunn and Paul Heaton. That was a handsome tribute to the company but, of necessity, only dealt with the last years in headline. This account seeks to mark the 20th anniversary of Palm Line's disappearance with some additional detail.

A rude shock
When I first sailed to West Africa, with Elder Dempster, we had to concede that, despite the 'lavatory brush' line jibes, Palm Line had the better looking vessels. Elders, for some apparent economy measure in 1964, then dispensed with the white upper parts of their ships' hulls and this - added to their dark brown masts, dumpy accommodation blocks and washed-out funnel colour - made them even duller birds when compared to the parrot-like finery of Palm Line. Mid-graphite grey and emerald green hulls, champagne masts, elegant superstructures and the distinctive shape and colour of their funnels gave plenty to admire. So my first ship to West Africa with Palm Line came as rather a rude shock when I found that I was back in the world of wooden hatchboards and tarpaulins. I should have remembered that the parent company of United Africa had a penchant for old technology as their steam lorries were often to be seen on the roads around Liverpool docks until late in the 1950s. The trade itself had also changed substantially even in the short time that I had been away and it was immediately apparent that any voyage profits would be hard to earn. The now-elderly *Ibadan Palm* was being loaded as a 'sweeper' service from Liverpool so we were berthed in Hornby Dock, far away from the familiar Canada Dock terminal, and only provided with cargo and the labour to load very intermittently. This was fine in that I was able to enjoy both Christmas and New Year at home but the downside was that we sailed with a deck crew signed on just before Christmas and therefore not one of the Shipping Federation's finest and faced a demanding itinerary of small parcels of cargo for virtually every port in West Africa between Dakar and the Congo.

It was the time when Nigerian ports were being besieged by ships loaded with bagged cement. The military dictatorship had allowed state governors to place their own contracts for materials and an armada of rustbuckets had flooded out of the Eastern Mediterranean and overwhelmed the country's port facilities. It was partly the reason why the *Ibadan Palm* was calling at so many of the other West African ports. She was needed to maintain the UK West Africa Lines (UKWAL) conference port calls in those countries disserviced by ships being delayed around Nigeria. The voyage was long by the standards of the route and the inadequacies of Palm Line's still good-looking but now very obsolete ships were cruelly exposed by the new demands of this always exacting trade. Just a few instances will serve to illustrate these

Ibadan Palm on the River Thames in April 1961. *[Ships in Focus]*

AFRICA PALM (2)
Warnowwerft, Warnemunde 1971;
10,008gt, 153 metres
Oil engine 2SCSA 8-cyl. by
Dieselmotorenwerke Rostock,
Rostock, 18.5 knots.

The Norwegian-flag *Joruna* was chartered to Palm Line as *Africa Palm* from 1974 to 1984, although for part of the last year she was subchartered as *Santa Barbara Pacific*. Subsequent

names were *Messaria, Tong Zhou, Dong Wan, Brilliant* and – most unlikely – *Luxury*. She was deleted from 'Lloyd's Register' in 1998. *[Ships in Focus]*

shortcomings. When the heavy tropical rain came, other ships soon had their MacGregor steel hatch covers put in place whilst we struggled with flapping canvas hatch tents. Whilst other ships had cranes or slewing derricks to pluck items out of wide hatches we had to re-rig our union purchase system every time we found an item of three tons or more and these were randomly distributed in the stow. Other ships had well-lit holds with few hiding places for the pilferer, we only had a few retro-fitted halogen deck lights and thus a continuous problem with shipboard criminals.

Replacement begins

Palm Line had only made a small start in re-equipping a fleet which was now the victim of block obsolescence. This unwelcome status of their fleet, legacy of an investment of £10 million for a twelve-ship series that ended in 1961, was painfully apparent. But now Palm Line was taking the second-hand option and, in 1974, had acquired the *Africa Palm* from Norwegian owners. A good-looking ship of a well-known East German standard type, she had a reasonable container capacity, a good turn of speed and large twin hatches with modern steel covers. She was taken over from her Norwegian owners in Singapore and then brought home to Liverpool with a full cargo of sugar in bulk from Mauritius.

In 1976 the company chartered the *Hasselburg* from Harald Schuldt of Hamburg and renamed her *Apapa Palm*. Only the bright green Palm Line funnel, however, relieved the dark brown drabness of her German owner's colours but she represented a major step towards accommodating the containers which were now appearing in significant numbers with cargo to West Africa. The ship was the fifth of an initial group of six B430 class ships built by the Polish shipyard of Stocznia Szczecinska Adolfo Warskiego in Szczecin, a yard that would later provide Palm Line's last ships.

The B430 was a ship type that was to become very well-known in the West African trade, for which it was well suited. It offered large twin hatchways, lower holds without too much run-in and 'tween decks without sides and so could load logs, packaged timber and bagged produce as easily as containers. In fact, the chartering of this ship was a tacit admission by Palm Line that they had earlier missed an opportunity in terms of harmonising their fleet with their UKWAL partners. Schuldts had already sold (in 1973/4) two of this class to Elder Dempsters who also chartered a third from the Hugo Stinnes fleet in 1976. When I was sailing with the Nigerian National Shipping Line (NNSL) in 1974 the word was that, after a couple of ill-judged second-hand purchases, the company would be buying one of the B430 class because a proposed sale to Palm Line had fallen through. This ship emerged later that year as the *River Hadejia*. The charter from German owners continued until the summer of 1977 when Palm Line made a decision to purchase but they then found that the *Hasselburg* itself was not for sale. In fact she was soon renamed *Hoegh Apapa* for another charterer and continued to trade to West Africa. Palm Line were offered instead the lead ship of the series, the *Schauenburg* (B430/1) and she proudly entered service in her full company livery in the autumn of 1977 as the second *Apapa Palm*.

B430 defects

It soon became apparent why she was the ship that her previous owners wished to sell as she was not wearing her four years of age well. The problems were most apparent on deck and arose from a combination of poor materials and skimped maintenance. It was clear that attractive export prices had disguised the fact that the quality of Polish and East German materials and equipment was quite inferior to those used in Western European yards. This meant that rust, the sailor's

RIVER HADEJIA
Stocznia Szczecinska, Szczecin, 1974;
9,389gt, 146 metres
Oil engine 2SCSA 6-cyl. H. Cegielski,
Poznan; 9,900 BHP, 17.5 knots
In the 1970s, Nigerian National Line

went to the same Polish builders as
Palm Line. This view of *River Hadejia*
on 24th April 1975 in the Thames
shows her impressive cargo gear.
    River Hadejia was sold in
1986, somewhat before Nigerian

National's collapse, and since then has
had a bewildering variety of names,
beginning with *Green Lagoon* and
ending with *Orient Ganges*, as which
she was broken up at Alang in 1999.
[J. and M. Clarkson]

APAPA PALM (2)
Stocznia Szczecinska, Szczecin, 1973;
9,413gt, 146 metres
Oil engine 2SCSA 8-cyl. H. Cegielski,
Poznan, 17 knots

The success of the B430 *Apapa Palm*
(1) led to her sister being bought, the
Schauenburg, confusingly also named
Apapa Palm (2) and seen above docking
at Liverpool on 14th May 1984. She was

sold to Venezuela in 1985 as *General
Salom*, and after six years as *Orient
Challenge* was broken up at Alang in
1999. *[J. and M. Clarkson]*

traditional enemy, had established itself well and the German crews had done little to prevent it. This was most apparent on the weatherdeck hatchcoamings where great undulations and corroded securing cleats made achieving watertightness a real problem. Then there were continuous difficulties with the hydraulic chain-drive for the hatchcovers due to the elongation of links as the steel distorted under strain. So the hatchcovers closed crabwise and then failed to seat properly: plenty of overtime for the carpenter but bad news for those trying to close up in a hurry. Poor steel also caused problems with the running gear aloft as block sheaves developed razor-sharp edges and then suffered collapsed bearings that allowed the sheaves to sway in the block and act as a very effective guillotine on the purchase wire running past. It did not always run, of course; it much preferred to twist itself into a huge single wire rope because the swivels to prevent that happening were equally defective. And then there was plenty of employment for the engineers on deck as flexible hydraulic hoses (despite their comprehensive replacement on purchase of the ship) had a frequent habit of bursting without having any warning leaks. And preferably when a consignment of expensive cocoa beans could be saturated with an oily mist. Soon I was reluctantly beginning to hanker after hatchboards and the rigmarole of derrick rigs when the very welcome news came that the company was to acquire two new buildings for delivery in 1979.

The news of these orders came in 1978, the year that three ships left the fleet by sale to new owners, these were the *Enugu Palm*, *Ibadan Palm* and *Katsina Palm*. The *Elmina Palm* had been sold in the autumn of 1977 and 1979 saw the departure of no less than four ships, the *Ilesha Palm*, *Ilorin Palm*, *Kano Palm* and *Lobito Palm*. So the fleet of a dozen ships that I had joined had almost halved to just seven within three years. It was therefore encouraging to join the *Bamenda*

Palm in Venice for familiarisation as she unloaded a full cargo of empty containers brought from her South Korean birthplace but West Africa's trade was continuing its steep downward trend. The first twenty years of independence for most of the countries there had been ones of continuous economic expansion, improvement in port facilities and generally peaceful trade. Now it was a sorry story of economic crisis, increasing poverty and the attendant consequences of deteriorating ports, acts of piracy at sea or in anchorages and theft and general lawlessness when alongside.

From Ulsan and Sunderland

The new *Badagry Palm* and *Bamenda Palm* were not exact sisters, as had been their predecessors in name, but were very similar in appearance and capability. Serving mainly on the latter ship, I was biased in her favour, but I still think that she was the better-looking vessel. The Ulsan yard of Hyundai produced a very attractive hull form from a nicely flared bow with prominent bulb to an elegant transom stern whilst the accommodation block aft was well-proportioned and furnished. The Sunderland-built ship was altogether more economical in appearance with a blunt stem, an equally blunt transom and those dreadful corrugations on the accomodation block that look more suited to the inside of a cofferdam. Most importantly, both ships had proper MacGregor steel hatchcovers and superior Velle cranes. Unfortunately, they both had plenty of void spaces around the squared holds to allow shipboard thieves to process their loot and the generous underdeck lighting was just the thing to supply the black market ashore in Ghana and elsewhere with fluorescent tubes.

Trading conditions in West Africa continued to deteriorate during 1980 and 1981. The cement ship queues had disappeared but easier access to berths did little to compensate as unloading a ship was becoming ever more

BADAGRY PALM (2)
Sunderland Shipbuilders Ltd., Sunderland, 1979; 12,279gt, 155 metres Oil engine 2SCSA 4-cyl. by Doxford Engines Ltd., Sunderland, 16.75 knots Palm's first newbuilding from Sunder-

land for 27 years did not have a long life with Palm: she was sold in 1986 to the Vlasov group who renamed her *Cordigliera*. After sale to Indian owners in 1995 she was unfortunate enough to be lost with her entire crew

on 13th December 1996 when water entered number 1 hold in bad weather whilst off South Africa. She was on a voyage from Durban to the Mediterranean with a cargo including steel and paper reels. *[Ships in Focus]*

BAMENDA PALM (2)
Hyundai Heavy Industries Ltd., Ulsan,
1979; 11,223gt, 150 metres
Oil engine 2SCSA 6-cyl. by Kawasaki
Heavy Industries Ltd., Kobe

Bamenda Palm was in service with
Palm Line until 1986, although for part
of this time she was chartered to Lloyd
Brasiliero as *Lloyd Texas*. Her list of
subsequent names is long: *Arko Glory,*

MC Ruby, Medipas Tide, MC Ruby
(three times), *Ville de Damas, Runner*
(twice), *CMBT Eagle, Renata* (twice),
and *African Star. [FotoFlite, Ashford]*

difficult. The containers were soon ashore and on their way
out of the port but then the problems began. General cargo
was naturally the magnet for thieves either operating within
the stevedoring labour or visiting as canoe pirates. Hired
guards with bows and arrows (!) and the use of fire hoses
helped to keep the seaward side of the ship safe but the
landward side was altogether more complicated. The dock
sheds were open for just a few daylight hours and then only
under the inducement of beer and cigarettes. Those cargoes
that could be discharged direct to road transport or safely
stored in the open were the only ones freely accepted for
landing. Dock labour and the ship's officers on duty spent
almost as much time sorting and shifting the cargo as actually
discharging it.

The Polish B181s

In the autumn of 1981 I joined the *Ikeja Palm* which was then
under charter to Anchor Line for a single outward voyage.
We wore the houseflag of our charterers but were otherwise
unchanged so the green palm tree was shown for the first time
in its history in the ports of Aden, Colombo, Karachi and
Bombay. This enjoyable escape to some peaceable but
traditional ports ended with the handing over of the ship to
her new owners in the roads off Piraeus. The *Lagos Palm* had
gone some weeks earlier so the year ended with the fleet now
reduced to just five ships. But at least it was now a very modern
fleet and the adding of the suffix *I* to the *Lagos Palm's* name
just prior to disposal was explained by Palm Line announcing
that the name would be revived in 1982 for one of the two
new ships soon to be delivered. The order had gone to Stocznia
Szczecinska and in fact the first ship was already launched.
They were part of another Harald Schuldt deal with the yard
and that firm would be providing some technical oversight of
the building. The ships were the fourth and fifth launchings

of the yard's B181 class, designated B181/II, and were
essentially larger versions of the earlier B430 type. The hope
was that, despite the very attractive dollar price (thought to be
just 10 million for the pair), we would buy rather better
materials this time and that at least we could apply good
maintenance to them from the start. So it was that a small
party of us travelled by road from Hamburg to Szczecin in the
summer of 1982. Poland was then under martial law and we
would not be immune from its effects even though we were
relatively insulated by staying in the city's main hotel. The
US dollar was the only means of payment for essentials so the
inflated black market rate for the zloty was rendered almost
meaningless. We made an initial faux pas by wearing our
pristine white Palm Line boiler suits in the shipyard. When
this raised hostile reactions it was explained to us that we might
be seen as boasting that we could buy detergents whilst the
Polish workers could not. The hotel manager chided us for
lowering the tone of his establishment by hanging our dun-
coloured working clothes out of the windows to dry. This was
to prevent theft and we countered by observing that the
Swedish drunks lying in the foyer every weekend morning
after enjoying the cheap pleasures of the city were hardly five-
star advertisements either. Far more serious to us was the
lack of any kind of external communication and the absolute
ban on the use of photocopiers. To make contact with London
other than by very terse telexes entailed a tiresome journey by
road to West Berlin. The DDR frontier, just a few miles up
the road from the hotel, was the place for for our car to be
practically dismantled regardless of the crossing direction. The
reason for this ordeal completely escaped our understanding,
surely this was a classic case of moving between the frying-
pan and the fire?

My task in the yard was to address the serious deck
maintenance issues which I knew had arisen with the B430

type. That meant making a comprehensive running overhaul plan and thus avoid building in future problems. The running gear for the Hallen-type derricks appeared to be only a little better in terms of quality but the hatch coverings were altogether more robust and simple to operate. The openings for No.3 hatch were to be the largest fitted in a British ship and so received close attention from both the DTI and Lloyd's Register (Schuldts normally used Germanischer Lloyd for classification). The dimensions of each hatch in the pair were around 110 feet by 30 feet so the hatch corners and the deck strengthening measures to compensate for these huge openings were very closely scrutinised. Fairly ominously, the watertightness of these covers was only achieved with a great deal of alteration and testing and we did experience some intermittent problems in service. I was concerned at the lubrication arrangements aloft for the derricks as they promised to be both vulnerable and difficult to access but little could be done about that. My other concern was underdeck security where the squared-off holds provided an even larger warren for concealing the criminal activities we would meet on our West African voyages. I wanted to have close-fitting padlocks and cage doors to seal off as many of these nooks and crannies as possible. The doors were no problem but I had to settle for much simpler padlocks in order to have a pass-key system. As there were so many other working spaces that needed to be secured, that measure was needed unless we were all to carry monstrous bunches of keys around. When we left the

yard I was quite happy that all of these corners were in apple-pie order as we had all been confined to our cabins for some hours before departure in order that the militia could ensure that we were free of stowaways.

The new *Lagos Palm* took up sailings within the UKWAL consortium for her maiden voyage but trade remained too poor to employ the *Lokoja Palm* when she was ready for service at the start of 1983. A quick paint job in Hull docks, however, and she emerged as the *Wameru* bearing the funnel colours of the Woermann Line, sailing for Hamburg to start a voyage charter to West Africa. It was in Hull that I received the first computer that I had ever laid hands on; it was designed to assist essential stability and draught calculations. It should have been a godsend as I had just covered reams of paper trying to come up with a figure for the maximum lift that we could take into Matadi without scraping the underside of a bridge that had just been put across the River Zaire. But the combination of being a computer novice aided only by a handbook that was rather less than comprehensive called for some intensive learning before I felt that I could trust the results.

A single voyage, with a homeward cargo mainly consisting of wet logs, took the shine off the gingerbread of our shiny new paintwork, sufficed for the Woermann connection and we then joined our sister ship in our traditional name and colours. But 1983 was a year of further worsening in West African trading conditions. Delmas and Hoegh were

LAGOS PALM (3)
Stocznia Szczecinska, Szczecin, 1982;
15,575gt, 177 metres
Oil engine 2SCSA 8-cyl. H. Cegielski,
Poznan, 17 knots

After just two years, *Lagos Palm* (3) was chartered to Lloyd Brasiliero as *Lloyd Rio*. On return she was briefly renamed *Lagos*, but was soon sold to

the USSR's Black Sea Shipping Company as *Boris Andreyev*. Her last reported change of name was to *Pearce* in 1996.

LOKOJA PALM (2)

Stocznia Szczecinska, Szczecin, 1982;
15,576gt, 177 metres
Oil engine 2SCSA 8-cyl. H. Cegielski,
Poznan, 17 knots
Delivered by the builders as the *Lokoja Palm* she sailed from Hull on her maiden voyage as the *Wameru* (right) but within months she reverted to her intended name (below). She then spent much of her brief career with Palm Line chartered out as *Lloyd Australia*. Briefly renamed *Lokoja* in 1986, later that year she too went to the USSR's Black Sea Shipping Company as *Mekhanik Bardetskiy*. She has subsequently carried the names *MSC Jamie*, *Jamie* and *MSC Buenos Aires*.

now using large ro-ros, Baco Liner had arrived with their novel barge carriers and less scrupulous operators were bribing their way through the chaos of most ports. The writing on the wall was our discovery that our corporate parent, the United Africa Company (UAC), was now chartering tonnage on their own account to avoid the delays experienced by the Conference lines attempting to stand apart from corrupt practices. The wheel of commerce that gave birth to Palm Line in 1949 (the end of UAC's dissatisfaction with the common carriers) had now come full circle.

So it was no great surprise when the *Lagos Palm* travelled across the South Atlantic to take on the name of *Lloyd Rio* and the colours of Lloyd Brasileiro (LB) in the early months of 1984. The *Africa Palm* had taken several months of the previous year to cruise the South Pacific in the Columbus Line of Hamburg's colours as the *Santa Barbara Pacific*. She was sold in 1984 for further trading, the *Lokoja Palm* became

the *Lloyd Australia* and the *Bamenda Palm* the *Lloyd Texas*. Only the *Apapa Palm* and *Badagry Palm* remained in the traditional Palm Line trades although, throughout this period, our single tanker, the *Matadi Palm*, ploughed her solitary furrow between West Africa and Europe with her oily cargoes, dedicated officers and a predominantly Spanish crew recruited from the international pool in Rotterdam.

Farewell to Palm

It was a refreshing change for most of Palm Line's sea staff to be away from the travails of West Africa even if those long and lonely southern ocean passages between Brazil and Australia took some getting used to. But, as 1985 went on, it was also apparent that the LB charters would move to cheaper ships and the *Bamenda Palm* was the first to leave. The same year also saw the admission by UAC that any active participation in the sea trade to West Africa was no longer of

MATADI PALM
Swan Hunter Shipbuilders Haverton Hill Shipyard, Haverton Hill; 1970, 8,870g, 148 metres
Oil engine 2SCSA 4-cyl. by Doxford

and Sunderland Ltd., Sunderland; 8,000 BHP, 15 knots
The vegetable oil tanker *Matadi Palm* is seen, also on the Thames, this time

on 7th July 1974. In 1985 her name was reduced to simply *Matadi*. As *Lian* she was broken up at Alang in November 1995. *[J. and M. Clarkson]*

any benefit to them and so the name, the palm tree trade mark and the shipping conference rights were all sold to the Ocean Group which already traded as Elder Dempster Lines and Guinea Gulf Line. The effective owner of the surviving former Palm Line ships became UAC International Limited and the Palm suffix was dropped from all the ships' names. It was intended that they should then fly the rather anodyne corporate houseflag of UAC and revert to the black-topped buff funnels of the original United Africa Company. But, in reality, the whole fleet was on the sale market and matters of economy and expediency reigned. The *Palm* suffix was painted out or erased but the funnels just lost their steel palm tree or current charterer's mark as hiring ended and purchasers emerged. The *Apapa Palm* went first (without losing her suffix) quickly followed as we went into 1986 by the rest of the fleet. I walked down the gangway of the *Lloyd Australia* in Rio de Janeiro late in March as the LB flag was being painted out on the funnel, flew home and never went to sea again.

So ended the 37-year existence of the real Palm Line, although the brand lived on another three years until purchased by the Groupe Delmas-Vieljeux and then disappeared from sight. The demise of the company was slightly different from that of other well-known British lines in that its business value was as part of the vertically integrated structure of Lever Brothers Ltd. Its life as a common carrier was unfortunately in an ocean trade that depended upon part of a continent that had descended into economic disarray. At the same time its corporate parent of Unilever was taking up the new business model of concentrating on core activities and being a shipowner was not one of them. Palm Line, for me, was a very happy company where everybody knew each other well and where a new recruit was immediately made welcome. The severance terms when it all had to end were very generous and the only surprise to me is that, although I still have contact with many former Palm Line colleagues, no formal reunion association was ever formed.

Lokoja Palm at Tilbury, one of the company's last ships.
[Newall Dunn collection]

TRAMPING INTO OBSCURITY
Steam's Indian summer on the Thames: Part 2
Roy Fenton

Charles Strubin and Co.

As a shipowner, Charles Strubin was in a different league from the others listed in these two articles: his fleet totalled around 30 vessels including Empires, Forts and a Liberty, all managed for the Ministry of War Transport. His career as a ship owner began in 1928 with old coasters, the *Oakford* (679/1900) and the Thames collier *Kilvey* (565/1904) in 1931. *Oakford* was wrecked off Vlieland, Holland in January 1934, her entire crew of ten being lost when the ship's boat capsized. *Kilvey* was broken up in 1935, and three large ships were then bought or taken into management. One of the managed ships was *Pomaron* (1,743/1899) which was nominally owned in Estonia. She was captured by a Spanish Nationalist cruiser in the Straits of Gibraltar in January 1938 and spent the rest of her long career under the Spanish flag. *Pomaron* had originally been the *Citrine*, largest ship in the fleet of William Robertson, Glasgow.

Expansion was rapid at the end of the 1930s, with larger ships and coasters entering the fleet. The latter began with *Jim* (833/1908) in 1939 and continued with a rush in 1940: *Polglen* (795/1915) followed by *Kalua* (722/1908), *Mons* (641/1919) and *Corrib* (624/1902). After a short break whilst a fleet of owned and managed deep-sea ships was built up, the coaster *Fleswick* (647/1899) arrived in 1945 from Culliford and Clark Ltd., suggesting a connection with the latter company, to whom *Corrib* had been sold in 1941, although surviving records listing directors do not confirm such a link. All the steam coasters were around 700 gross tons, and almost certainly used in the East Coast coal trade into London. Indeed, *Kalua* was sunk by the Luftwaffe whilst on a voyage in this trade during April 1941. Two former Dutch steamers, *Helmond* (983/1921) and *Haarlem* (970/1917), were bought from Culliford and Clark in 1945. Few vessels stayed long in the fleet: *Mons* was sold in 1942, the Dutch pair went in 1947, and *Fleswick* was disposed of to Greek owners after just 18 months. *Jim* became a rather bizarre, though tragic, casualty: sunk in March 1945 near Orfordness by what is believed to have been a midget submarine. Longest resident in the fleet was *Polglen* which, having survived from 1940 to 1945, became a casualty of war when she hit a stray mine and sank off Borkum in May 1948, terminating Strubin's interest in coasters. Larger ships continued to be managed or owned until 1949. Typical of these small shipping companies was the modest capitalisation of Charles Strubin and Co. Ltd. – just over £3,000 in 1946, with all but £1 in the hands of Charles Strubin himself.

The company's funnel colours were black basic with a white band on which was a large blue diamond bearing the letter S in white. Two versions of a houseflag are recorded, one identical to the funnel band, the other plain blue with a white letter S.

George Tom and Co. Ltd.

This company had only seven ships, but managed to create an interesting fleet during its nine-year existence. The first acquisition came in 1942, the *J.F.V.* (515/1909), which had started life with Spillers the millers as *Wheatfield*. In 1943 came the *Silverthorn* (439/1908), whose interest lies in being sold back to a previous owner, S. William Coe and Co. Ltd., when Tom had finished with her in 1946. For his next acquisitions, Tom used United Coasters Ltd. as a vehicle, and this had a dedicated naming scheme: the little *Rivelin* (365/1919) became the *Stratton Lea* in 1946, and the former Kennaugh steamer *Skelwith Force* (592/1908) the *Stratton Downs*. Now began the surprises, with another owning company, Regent Shipping Co. Ltd., buying the armed trawler HMS *Juliet* in 1947 and sending her to Grimsby where she was slipped, lengthened, re-engined with a Crossley diesel, and renamed *Peterjon* (585/1941). This gave them a relatively new and presumably cheap motor

The policy pursued with illustrating this article is to show vessels only in the colours and name used by the featured owner. *Kilvey* was bought by Charles Strubin in March 1931 and was photographed on the Thames in December 1932, before Strubin had added a blue diamond and a white letter S to his funnels. Her unusual profile tells of an interesting history. She was built on the Tyne as *Bow* for the Commercial Gas Company, who needed colliers which could negotiate Bow Creek and the River Lea to serve its Poplar Gas Works, and her funnel and masts were hinged to allow her to pass beneath Barking Road Bridge. She was sold in 1926 and renamed *Kilvey*, and after a series of short-lived owners and at least one sale by the Admiralty Marshall ended her life with Strubin, who sold her to breakers in Ghent during 1935. *[R. Snook/F.W. Hawks]*

Even allowing for the inferior nature of the print, *Peterjon* shows little evidence of her origin as the Shakesperian-class Admiralty trawler HMS *Juliet*. In April 1951 the motor coaster was sold by Regent Shipping Co. Ltd. to the Limerick Steam Ship Co. Ltd. which renamed her *Plassy* and subjected her to further modification to become a reefer. On her regular run from Liverpool to Galway, *Plassy* ran aground on Finnis Rock in the Aran Islands on 8th March 1960. [Roy Fenton collection]

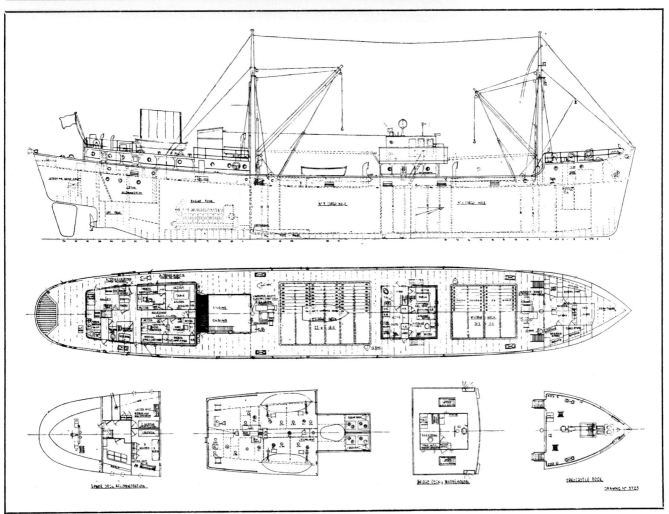

GENERAL ARRANGEMENT DRAWINGS OF THE " PETERJON "

coaster, but later that year United Coasters Ltd. acquired a seriously old one, the *Innisshannon* (238/1913) which it renamed *Stratton Croft*. The histories of the pioneering group of motor coasters to which she belonged were covered in 'Record' 26. Then it was back to ageing steamers for the Tom fleet, with the big coaster *Kilworth* (803/1911) bought in 1950 from Grand Union (Shipping) Ltd. by yet another company, Fenchurch Shipping Co. Ltd., and renamed *Fenchurch* in 1951, the earlier ship of that name having departed the fleet in 1948. But within a few months of renaming, *Fenchurch* and the other remaining vessel,

Peterjon, were sold, and Tom's ship owning and management came to a sudden end. His company managed the unusual feat of neither losing a ship nor having to sell one to breakers, and all vessels found further owners, despite their considerable age. However, Tom's precipitous departure from business left little trace other than entries in register books. No funnel markings of United Coasters Ltd. are known, no photographs of the *Stratton* ships under these names have been found, and nor can we guess at any geographical connection which might have inspired this naming scheme. Obscurity indeed.

On the funnel of *Themsleigh* can be discerned a broad, white-edged band (probably red) carrying a diamond (probably blue) with the white letters T E S for Tyson, Edgar Shipping Ltd. – the only record found of this owner's funnel. The steamer had been built in 1915 for Richard Hughes as *Joffre Rose* and survived an incident in May 1941 when she was beached in Dale Roads, Milford Haven following an attack by the Luftwaffe off St. David's Head whilst on a voyage from Dublin to Newport in ballast. She was sold to the Holderness Steamship Co. Ltd., Hull as *Holdernene* in October and became *Themsleigh* in 1952. She was broken up at Dunston-on-Tyne by Clayton and Davie Ltd. in late 1955. *[Roy Fenton collection]*

Tyson, Edgar Shipping Ltd.

Almost last alphabetically, Tyson, Edgar were definitely the final one of this selection of London companies to begin ship owning, in 1949, and they had the honour of being the very last owner of each of their five ships, all of which went from them to the breakers, often within a year of acquisition. *Firethorn* (321/1903) began operations when she was bought by Douglas Edgar in June 1949, being soon transferred to Tyson, Edgar Shipping Ltd. *Themston* (711/1904) came a year later, and its name seems to have inspired the renaming of the next acquisition, *Holdernene* (715/1915) becoming *Themsleigh*, a rare example of someone buying a ship from the Holderness Steamship Co. Ltd., which usually ran its ships until they were fit only for the breakers. With the *Galacum* (585/1915), bought in September 1951, a different naming scheme was used and she became *Satco Prefect* in the managed Satco Shipping Co. Ltd. The same owning company took the *Croham* (391/1912) in December 1951, soon renaming her *Satco Minor*. *Satco Prefect* was the last to go to the breakers, arriving on the Tyne in April 1954.

Wirral Shipping Co. Ltd.

It is not known whether Henry Elmer had any connections with the Cheshire peninsula, but in late 1947 he bought two coasters which he registered in the ownership of the Wirral Shipping Co. Ltd. which was firmly based in London. A change of heart – or the correction of a clerical error – saw this become the Wirral Steamship Co. Ltd. in early 1948. *Wirral Bank* (373/

Before her purchase by the Wirral Shipping Co. Ltd. in 1947, *Wirral Bank* (373/1906) had previously been *City of Malines* and before that *Prince Leopold*, both owned by companies operating a service between London to Brussels. With her bridge amidships she was an ungainly-looking, bluff-bowed tub, possibly because of the constraints of the canals leading to the Belgian capital. In January 1951 she was sold by the Midland Bank to a Norman Dakin of London and although renamed *Segura* was broken up at Grays, Essex within 18 months. *[Ships in Focus]*

1906) had previously been *City of Malines* and before that *Prince Leopold*, both owned by companies operating a service between London and Brussels. With her bridge amidships, she was an ungainly-looking craft: possibly because of the constraints of the canals leading to the Belgian capital. The tiny *Wirral Cape* (143/1897) had previously been *Fawn*, built for Guernsey owners but subsequently owned in the Isle of Man and elsewhere. Elmer did not prosper, however. In January 1951 the *Wirral Bank* was sold by the Midland Bank, suggesting they had foreclosed on her mortgage, and the *Wirral Cape* went to breakers in March 1951.

London-Greeks and London-others

The many Greek shipowners who made London their base were mainly involved in operating deep-sea tramps and tankers, but a couple qualify for inclusion in this feature by virtue of owning coasters.

The delightfully named Jenny Steamship Co. Ltd. had been established in London during 1938 by sons of John G. Livanos. It bought mainly cargo liners, tramps and large colliers to which it gave names beginning 'River', but its coasters were treated differently. William Robertson's *Tourmaline* (835/1898) was bought in 1938, renamed *Bawtry* early in 1939 and quickly transferred to the eponymous Bawtry Steamship Co. Ltd. She was bombed and sunk during the Dunkirk evacuation, but later raised by the Germans and returned to service. An oddity was the Dutch-built *South Coaster* (513/1916), which never traded for the company. On 13th December 1943 she had run shore at Pole Sands, Exmouth Bar whilst on a voyage from Garston to Exmouth with coal. In April 1944 she was sold as a constructive total loss to the Jenny Steamship Co. Ltd., but salvage attempts were

unsuccessful and in 1951 she was sold to be broken up in situ. Even this operation was inconclusive, as her remains are still visible from trains along the former Great Western Railway's mainline along the Devonshire coast.

A.G. Tsavliris Ltd. began ship owning in London in 1940, and confused future historians and photograph collectors by insisting on using the name *Granny Suzanne* over and over again, often for aged tramps making one last voyage to the breakers. Just one coaster was so treated, the former *Jolly Guy*, *Gorselands* and *Springwave* (503/1918) which came to a sad end, sunk in collision with the Panamanian steamer *San Miguel* (472/76) in February 1949 three miles south east of the South Goodwin Light Vessel whilst on a voyage from Blyth to Dover with a cargo of coal. Tsavliris used several other naming schemes, including family names followed by the initial T. *Claire T* (439/1912) was formerly *Harptree Coombe* bought in 1947 and traded until 1951 when she was broken up at Gateshead. *George T* (904/1922) had carried a variety of names since being built at East Cowes as *Allerton*, and had last been with Comben Longstaff as *Surreybrook*. In 1952 she was sold to owners in Greece. Strictly speaking, Tsavliris should not be included in this review, as the family were anything but short-lived owners, even under the British flag, which they continued to use for some of their deep-sea tramps until well into the 1960s.

Although they were definitely short-lived, it is probably wrong to classify T. and W. Colassi Ltd. as London-Greeks. The company was under the wing of Purvis Shipping Co. Ltd., which had strong links with owners from the Eastern Mediterranean and Black Sea. For the coasters which Colassi bought in 1946 they got as far as proposing a naming scheme, although it was not a unique one. Although at least one

This photo of *Claire T* from a slightly damaged negative shows her slipped at an unidentified yard: does any reader recognise it from its distinctive craneage? The 1912-built steamer was now on her fourth name, having been built at Aberdeen for local owners as *Norah Elsmie*, sold to become *Cromwell* in 1917, *Harptree Combe* for Ald Shipping in 1926, becoming *Claire T* for A.G. Tsavliris Ltd. in July 1947. She arrived at Gateshead for breaking up by J.J. King and Co. on 13th March 1951. *[G.E. Brownell/World Ship Society Ltd.]*

reputable source lists two ships as being renamed, these names were not formally registered. *City of Malines* (373/1906) was to be renamed *Colhill* according to the usually well informed 'Lloyd's Confidential Index' for June 1947, but as we saw earlier she was sold in October 1947 to become *Wirral Bank*. Similarly the *Harptree Coombe* (439/1912) bought in July 1946 is listed as becoming *Coldene*, but her official registration papers deny this, maintaining that she was sold to Tsavliris in July 1947 still carrying the name she had inherited from Ald Shipping Ltd. of Bristol. Quite possibly, names beginning 'Col' were rejected because similar names were being used by another fleet, that of Coastwise Colliers Ltd. No proposed name is shown for Colassi's *Palmston* (430/1907), which was sold to Denmark in 1947. *Palmston* had been built in Scotland as *La Plata* for an Argentine company, returning to the UK to be renamed in 1917. After 1947 T. and W. Colassi Ltd. disappear from lists of ship owners.

One steamer only

To round off this review are a group of London-based one-steamer companies which, if anything, are even more obscure than those already catalogued. Ernest F. Coe bought the Workington-built coaster *Slateford* (355/1903) in 1941. The only connection with the Liverpool-based S.William Coe and Co. Ltd. – itself an operator of superannuated steam – was the January 1944 sale of *Slateford* to the Liverpool company's subsidiary, Ribble Shipping Co. Ltd. Neither was Coe Line Ltd. associated with either of the other Coe companies. Its sole steamer was *Coe-Pam* ex *Weston* (485/1920) owned from 1947-1952. Unusually amongst the companies listed here, it also had a motor coaster from 1946 to 1950, the *Coe-Jean* (410/1944), one of the ungainly, prefabricated Empire F type, ex-*Empire Factor*. Deepdene Steamship Co. Ltd. bought the former John Kelly Ltd. collier *Cushendun* (646/1904) from other London owners in 1945, but did not rename her. That this company had London-Greek owners is suggested by the management of its ship by an organisation well-connected in

Greece, P. Wigham-Richardson and Co. Ltd., which association continued when its ship went under the Greek flag in 1946. The sole ship owned by Falconer Coasters Ltd. from 1928 to 1953, the *Graham F* (294/1920), was illustrated in the previous part of this feature. Last in this list is the steamer *Arild* (518/1920), acquired early in 1952 by Risted and Nerdrum Ltd., with both ship's and owner's name hinting at a Norwegian connection. The owners restyled themselves Nerdrum Shipping Ltd. in 1954, and proposed renaming their steamer *Norbury* to match, but this did not happen and she was sold to Greece in 1955. Nerdrum Shipping Ltd. went on to greater things, and are listed as owning two German-built bulk carriers, *Lewis R. Sanderson* and *William M. Currie* (both 11,416/1956) until 1964.

The sale of *Arild* to Greece in 1955 coincided with the end of the era of ageing steam coasters being able to make a living in British coastal and short-sea trades. A small fleet of these vintage craft could be bought for the price of a new motor coaster, and with cargoes plentiful could probably earn just as much, even if their operation was much less efficient. Age, imminence of special surveys, difficulty of finding engineers and especially firemen thinned their numbers during the 1950s, but the cull became almost total once freight rates began to fall in 1955, and only a very few coastal steamers hung on until the 1960s, mostly owned in Hull or Liverpool.

Lest anyone cry that there has been an important omission of a London company from these articles, Springwell Shipping Co. Ltd., the author maintains that this was a company in an altogether bigger league, with a more extensive fleet which ordered new steamers and motor vessels (its fleet included the *Springfjord* (2,036/1940) mentioned in 'Record' 32). This is not to say that this organisation with its network of subsidiaries or managed companies (often difficult to distinguish) does not deserve coverage, but whoever chooses to work on it has the amusing task of untangling its ownership and policy. Needless to say, the editors would be delighted to hear from anyone willing to do this for Springwell or any other company listed in this feature.

The *Coe-Pam* was well photographed between 1947 and 1952, and here she is at Preston, note the distinctive painting of her bridge front. Her funnel colours are recorded as black with a representation of the houseflag, itself carrying blue, white, red, white and blue bands, over which was a black letter C. In 1952 *Coe-Pam* was sold to W.N. Lindsay of Leith who renamed her *Mistley*. She sank in June 1957 after striking Reefdyke Rocks off North Ronaldsay whilst on a voyage to Fair Isle with coal. *[J. and M. Clarkson]*

Arild had been built in 1920 by a yard not noted for its coaster building, Swan, Hunter and Wigham Richardson Ltd. of Wallsend, and had an unusual hull form, with a forecastle but no raised quarter deck. Her appearance is not enhanced by the tripod mast built on her funnel in the upper photograph. The lower shows this positioned on the deckhouse aft, but no less subject to smoke. Earlier names were *Alfred Harrison* until 1930, *Broomlands* until 1946,

*Polurria*n until 1947 and *Rifsnes* until she was bought by Risted and Nerdrum Ltd. in 1952. The funnel is black with a white panel on which are three red St. Andrews' crosses, interrupted by a red-outlined white oval with letters R & N in red. *Arild* was sold to Greek owners in May 1955 to become *Aspasia*, and fitting of a oil engine in the late 1950s helped her ensure her survival, latterly as *Marilena*, until broken up in 1971. *[Upper: World Ship Society Ltd.; lower: Charles Hill]*

SOURCES AND ACKNOWLEDGEMENTS

We thank all who gave permission for their photographs to be used, and for help in finding photographs we are particularly grateful to Tony Smith, Jim McFaul and David Whiteside of the World Ship Photo Library; to Ian Farquhar, Fred Hawks, Peter Newall, William Schell, George Scott; and to David Hodge and Bob Todd of the National Maritime Museum, and other museums and institutions listed. Research sources have included the *Registers* of William Schell and Tony Starke/Rodger Haworth, *Lloyd's Register*, *Lloyd's Confidential Index*, *Lloyd's War Losses*, *Mercantile Navy Lists*, *Marine News* and *Shipbuilding and Shipping Record*. Use of the facilities of the World Ship Society, the Guildhall Library, the Public Record Office and Lloyd's Register of Shipping are gratefully acknowledged. Particular thanks also to Heather Fenton for indexing work, and to Marion Clarkson for accountancy services.

Photographer in Focus
DAVID de MAUS - Part 2
Ian Farquhar

TARANAKI (above)
Blackwood and Gordon, Port Glasgow,
1865, 415gt, 186.5 x 24.8 x 13.9 feet
C. 2-cyl., 90 NHP
Prior to the establishment of the Union
Steam Ship Company of New Zealand
in 1875, the principal shipping
company operating on the New
Zealand coast was the New Zealand
Steam Shipping Co. Ltd. of Wellington,
which had been reorganised from the
New Zealand Steam Navigation Co.
Ltd. in 1871. The *Taranaki* is shown at
Port Chalmers in New Zealand Steam
Shipping Company colours of white
funnel with black top, black hull and
pink boot-topping. The company was
taken over by the Union Company in
1876 and *Taranaki* had two years
under its ownership before being
wrecked near Tauranga on 29th
November 1878, after a short career of
13 years.

TAIAROA (opposite top right)
A. and J. Inglis, Glasgow, 1875; 438gt,
189.3 x 23.2 t x 12.6 feet

C. 2-cyl. by A and J. Inglis, Glasgow
Although feeder ship is something of a
modern term, the steamer *Taiaroa* was
sent out to Port Chalmers from
Glasgow in 1875 to be employed as
such, working between other South
Island ports feeding cargo to the
Albion Line sailing ships which
sometimes remained in Port Chalmers
for up to three months waiting to
secure a full return cargo. She may
well have been the only steamer
owned by the Albion Shipping
Company of Glasgow. By the time she
arrived the newly formed Union Steam
Ship Company of New Zealand Ltd.
had greatly improved coastal shipping
services in and out of Port Chalmers
and this company purchased the
Taiaroa seven months later. The
name Taiaroa is taken from the landfall
headland at the entrance to Otago
Harbour and came from the name of
one of the early Maori chiefs in the
area. *Taiaroa* was later employed on a
mail contract from Sydney to Noumea
and also in the Fiji trade before being

wrecked on the South Island of New
Zealand's Kaikoura Coast on 11th April
1886.

ROTOMAHANA (opposite bottom
right)
William Denny and Brothers,
Dumbarton, 1879; 1,727gt, 298.2 x
35.2 x 23.7 feet
C. 2-cyl. by Denny and Co.,
Dumbarton
The fine lines of *Rotomahana* are
shown in this photograph as the ship
passes Port Chalmers. Walter Brock
of William Denny and Brothers and
John Darling, the Union Company
engineer in Scotland, designed the
steamer which the 'Lennox Herald',
Dumbarton described as 'the finest
specimen of the shipbuilder and
engineer's skill that has been turned
out by Denny Bros., her builders, and
Denny and Company, who constructed
her machinery.' She was the first
ocean-going steamer in the world built
entirely of mild steel and her standing
bowsprit and sleek lines gave her an

"TAIAROA"

impression of speed that captured the imagination of the travelling public of Australia and New Zealand. On her trials she made over 15 knots. She had accommodation for 100 passengers in first class and 70 in second and was mainly employed on the high-profile trans-Tasman service but from 1897 she finally transferred to the service she had been designed for – the overnight passage between Lyttelton and Wellington. She was described as the Union Company's 'fancy boat' and later as the 'greyhound of the Pacific' and carried a gilded greyhound on her main mast. After 41 years' service she was laid up in 1920 and sold for scrapping in 1925. The partially dismantled hull was scuttled off Port Phillip Heads, Victoria on 29th May 1928.

ROTOMAHANA (right)

Officers and crew of the *Rotomahana* line the foredeck while the vessel was under repair in dry dock at Port Chalmers, following an incident on 4th August 1883 when she bumped heavily on Waipapa Reef, Southland and required extensive repairs to her stern post and bottom plates which had been set up. Had she been built of iron instead of steel it is likely she would have remained on the reef. The raked bow and the figurehead of a Maori maiden can be seen, as well as elaborate scrollwork. The legendary master of the vessel, Michael Carey, is fourth from right.

SAMOA (below)

T. Wingate and Co., Whiteinch, Glasgow, 1878; 1,096gt, 245.1 x 30.0 x 14.2 feet
C. 2-cyl. by T. Wingate and Co., Whiteinch.
1903: T. 3-cyl. by Kawasaki Dockyard Co., Kobe.

In 1875 McMeckan, Blackwood and Company of Melbourne took delivery of two new steamers specially designed for their trans-Tasman service. At the time McMeckan, Blackwood had effective control of this trade. The first of the pair, *Ringarooma*, arrived Melbourne in August 1875 and her sister *Arawata* three months later. Within three years McMeckan, Blackwood was taken over by the Union Steam Ship Company of

New Zealand and *Ringarooma* remained with that company until she was laid up at Port Chalmers in March 1891. For the next ten years she lay idle until she was sold to A. Kunst of Samoa, who extensively overhauled the ship and renamed her *Samoa*. The illustration shows *Samoa* just prior to her departure for Samoa on 10th April 1901. The Samoan venture was not successful and the ship was sold to Japanese owners in July 1901 and renamed *Geiho Maru*. Re-engined in 1903 she served under several Japanese owners until she foundered in December 1913.

UNION STEAM SHIP COMPANY CHRISTMAS CARD (opposite top)

De Maus made this montage in 1883 as the Christmas card for the head office staff of the Union Steam Ship Company of New Zealand Ltd. In addition to featuring eleven of the company's larger passenger ships, along with insets of their masters, it also shows the Dunedin Head Office building as well as a portrait of James Mills, the Managing Director of the company.

SHIRE LINE MONTAGE (opposite bottom)

Six Shire Line ships of Turnbull, Martin and Company feature on this de Maus

photographic montage which shows all the company's ships in the New Zealand trade. *Fifeshire* first came to Port Chalmers in January 1888 and the other five vessels followed – *Nairnshire* in 1889, *Morayshire* in 1890 and *Buteshire, Banffshire* and *Perthshire* in 1895. The line became part of the Federal-Houlder-Shire line consortium in the Australian and New Zealand trades from 1904 to 1912 and its Australian trade assets were acquired by Clan Line in 1918.

MIOWERA (above)
C.S. Swan and Hunter, Newcastle-upon-Tyne, 1892; 3,393gt, 345.0 x 42.2 x 25.1 feet
T.3-cyl. by Wallsend Slipway and Engineering Co. Ltd., Wallsend
Melbourne shipowner James Huddart decided to go head to head with the Union Steam Ship Company on the trans-Tasman trade and in 1892 had two elaborate passenger ships built – *Warrimoo* and *Miowera*. The vessels were registered to a separate company – New Zealand and Australasian Steam Ship Co. Ltd. – in which Huddart Parker Ltd. had a quarter share. Each had accommodation for 233 passengers in first class, 127 in second class and no expense was spared in the fitting out. *Miowera* on her second voyage from Sydney to Auckland created a new record of 3 days 10 hours and 52 minutes between the two ports. After a fierce battle for market share with the

Union Company the ships were switched to a new Pacific run as the Canadian Australian Royal Mail Line. They were sold to New Zealand Shipping Company in 1899 and the Union Company became joint managers. *Miowera* was sold to the Union Company in 1908 and renamed *Maitai*. While on passage from San Francisco to Wellington she was wrecked on a reef at Avarua, Rarotonga on Christmas Day 1916.

A portion of the ornate and costly interiors of the ships is shown in this de Maus photograph of the grand saloon in *Miowera* while the other photograph features the social hall and music room.

WARRIMOO (below)
C.S. Swan and Hunter, Newcastle-upon-Tyne, 1892; 3,326gt, 345.0 x 42.2 x 25.1 feet
T. 3-cyl. by Wallsend Slipway and Engineering Co. Ltd., Newcastle-upon-Tyne

Miowera's sister-ship *Warrimoo* is shown berthed at Port Chalmers in October 1892. She is in the colours of the New Zealand and Australasian Steam Ship Company, with a black-topped, creamy-white funnel, on which was a blue cross with the stars of the Southern Cross picked out on it in gold. Like her sister, *Warrimoo* was sold to New Zealand Shipping Company in 1899 and the Union Steam Ship Company brought her outright in 1901. She was sold to Khiam Yik and Company of Singapore in 1916 and was lost when in collision with an escorting destroyer off the coast of Tunisia on 18th May 1918.

WAKATIPU (bottom)
William Denny and Bros., Dumbarton, 1876; 1,797gt. 290.0 x 33.1 x 24.0 feet
C. 2-cyl. by Denny and Co., Dumbarton.
1891: Q. 4 cyl. by Denny and Co. Dumbarton.

Described by Peter Denny as an 'Australian and New Zealand clipper' *Wakatipu* was built as a speculation as iron was cheap and she made history for the Union Company by inaugurating the first Trans Tasman service of the company. She sailed from Dunedin 4th October 1876 for Sydney via Lyttelton, Wellington, Nelson and Hokitika. At the time of her launching she was the largest vessel ever built for the New Zealand trade. Initially the 64 shares were owned by Peter Denny (36), John Darling (16), the Union Company Superintendent engineer, James Galbraith (8) of P. Henderson and her master, Captain Angus Cameron (4) but in 1878 Union Company took full ownership. She remained on Tasman service for 22 years and was then placed in the Sydney-Launceston trade from 1899 to 1921. She was laid-up in Sydney until 1924 when she was sold for demolition. However, after being partially dismantled the hull was sold to BHP for use as a tar storage vessel at the Port Waratah steelworks. Over time the tar collected on the one side of the hull and she was in danger of capsizing. She was scrapped in 1930 after a career of 54 years afloat. In the photograph the *Wakatipu* is shown at Port Chalmers in 1891, after she had been re-engined and extensively overhauled. A unique feature of the ship for those early times was a deeptank with a capacity for 320 tons of water ballast or cargo. It was thought this would be of value if she was engaged in the coal trade with the tank being filled with water to provide better stability in light condition.

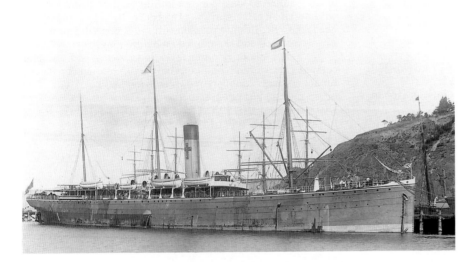

PUTTING THE RECORD STRAIGHT

Letters, additions, amendments and photographs relating to features in *any* issues of 'Record' are welcomed. Letters may be edited. Communications by e-mail are welcome, but senders are asked to include their postal address. Items received following the article on Palm Line in 'Record' 35 have been held over until the next issue, as comments are expected on the continuation of the story which appears in this issue.

At Foyers

I read with interest the items on Foyers Jetty, Loch Ness. I am fairly certain that the steam coaster shown on page 55 of 'Record' 33 is *Loch Etive*, 237 tons gross, port of registry Glasgow, built in April 1910 by Scott and Sons, Bowling.

The ship traded for years with alumina from the company's plant at Larne to the refinery at Foyers via the Caledonian Canal and return cargoes of coal usually from Ayr. She was manned by a crew from the Larne area who sailed with the ship for years. She was well kept and money was not spared which explains her long and trouble free life of 46 years. I believe she was built to fit the locks in the canal, hence the overall length of only 122 feet. During my apprenticeship, I worked on *Loch Etive's* two-furnace Scotch boiler and her compound steam engine, winch and steering engine.

JOHN MCCARLIE, Newcastle, New South Wales, Australia.
The history of Loch Etive *appears below. Ed.*

LOCH ETIVE (2) 1910-1956
O.N. 129484 237g 89n
122.3 x 21.6 x 9.4 feet
C. 2-cyl. by Fisher's Ltd., Paisley.
4.1910: Completed by Scott and Son, Bowling (Yard No. 220) for John G. Stewart, Glasgow as LOCH ETIVE.
1916: Sold to the British Aluminium Co. Ltd. (P.D. Hendry and Sons, managers), Glasgow.
1950: Sold to John Rainey Ltd., Larne.

26.3.1956: Arrived at Dublin to be broken up by the Hammond Lane Foundry Ltd.

Empire Mayring

No photo was found for the *Islamabad ex-Empire Mayring* in the article 'Under the Star and Crescent' in 'Record' 35 (page 167), so I am sending you prints of the builder's trials photographs. I was the Naval Architect at Cochrane Shipbuilders from mid-1960s until closure in 1992 and as the unofficial archivist had my own small collection of surplus-to-requirements photographs of ships of my period at the yard along with a selection of earlier vessels. The yard records show the *Empire Mayring* being delivered in January 1946 and her sister *Empire Mayrover* in May 1946.

ERIC HAMMAL, 16 Red Oak Lane, Stannington, Sheffield S66 BF11

My family have owned and run a grain trading firm, W.N. Lindsay Ltd., since 1864 and it thrives to this day. From the 1920s to 1979 they also owned a number of coasters, latterly under the banner W.N. Lindsay (Shipowners) Ltd. According to my father, they were asked to manage the *Empire Mayring* from the builder's yard until a buyer could be found for her.

Now our shipping business carted the usual bulk cargoes: grain, coal, gravel. A small 'tweendecker was not terribly suited to such cargoes and my father grumbled that working small parcels of bulk in and out of her was a continuous headache. So, despite pressure from the government to buy her, we refused and she moved on before long.

The photo is quite revealing. She is still broadly equipped for wartime conditions but it looks like our company's funnel colours – orangey-red, blue band and black top. The blue band can just be discerned.

DOUGLAS J. LINDSAY, 3 Rectory Court, Old Banwell Road, Locking, Weston-super-Mare BS24 8BS.

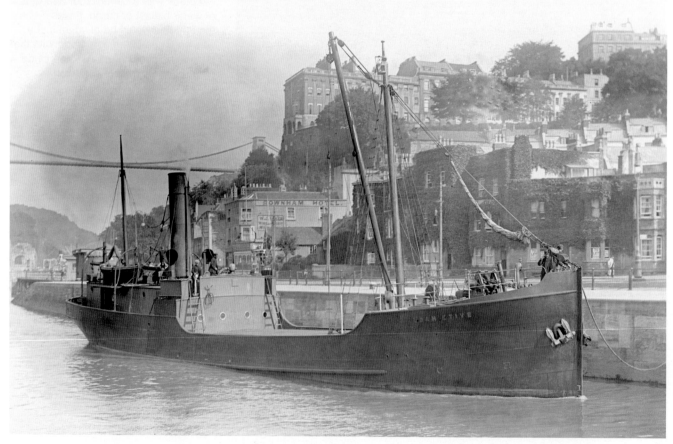

Loch Etive in the Avon: note the furled foresail. *[J. and M. Clarkson]*

Empire Mayring on trials in the Humber during January 1946, probably off Riverside Quay. Douglas Lindsay also kindly lent us a copy of the upper photograph. *[Eric Hammal collection]*

Department of Correction

Going all the way back to page 5 of 'Record' 1, I believe the reference to U 160 in the caption to *Armadale* should have read U 60. A.J. Tennent in his 'British Merchant Ships sunk by U-boats in the 1914-18 War' listed her as being sunk by U 60. Recourse to 'German Warships of World War 1' published by Ian Allan revealed that U 160 was not completed until sometime in 1918, while U 60 was completed in 1916 and survived to surrender in November 1918. Clearly then it must have been U 60 which sank *Armadale* on 27th June 1917. I surmise that the location of 160 miles north west of Tory Island given by Tennent could have been confused with the U-boat's number.

ROBERT H. LANGLOIS, Feu Follet, Maisons au Compte, Vale, Guernsey GY3 5HF

An error in 'Record' 25 which has not so far been picked up by your eagle-eyed readers: *Taipooshan* (ex *Apapa*) is not at anchor, she is approaching a buoy and her port anchor chain can be seen to be broken out and hung off ready for securing to the buoy. The people boarding are probably work gangs from the nearby walla-wallas.

E.E. MILBURN, 62 Abbots Way, Preston Farm, Tynemouth, Tyne and Wear NE29 8LX.

In 'Record' 10 I stated that the first *John Holt*, later *Garthorpe*, had been sold to U.S.S.R. and had been renamed *Anatoli Serov*. I also recorded her as having sunk in the Black Sea after striking a floating mine in 1949, an event reported in March 1951.

In May 2002 the 'Merseylog' of the World Ship Society featured photographs of the *Anatoli Serov* taken in Siberia about December 2001 by Nikolay Pritulyak. The ship is, without doubt, the former *John Holt*. She has been a fish transport with the USSR fishing fleet and registered at Petropavlovsk-Kamchatskiy.

Unfortunately the person who down loaded the photos from the Internet did not save them. Apparently it was featured on the Thames Ship Society website but is no longer there. I would be very grateful if any reader can please forward to me the photos from the net.

GEOFF HOLMES, 17 Bayswater Court, Newport Avenue, Wallasey, Cheshire CH45 8QJ gomezholmes@excite.com

Bristol City Line follow up

Richard Ardern gives details of the photograph showing a pristine Gloucester City *(4) of 1954 on page 14 of 'Record' 33. It shows her off Dover having dropped the North Sea Pilot during her delivery voyage from South Shields to Bristol. Richard's great uncle, George Birkby, Bristol City Line's Marine Superintendent, was on board. His detailed notes on her trials, delivery voyage and reception in Bristol indicate that the photograph was taken on or about 26th September 1954.*

All about the *City of Sydney*

The article on David de Maus in Ships in Focus 'Record' 35 includes photographs of the Pacific Mail Steamship Company's sister ships *City of San Francisco* and *City of New York*. As identified, both these vessels were completed in 1875 at the Chester, Pennsylvania yard of John Roach and Sons. There were, in fact, three sister ships, the third being *City of Sydney* of 3,016gt, also being completed in 1875.

The losses of the first two vessels are described in the article but the third vessel continued to sail long after the first two were lost. The *City of Sydney* was purchased by the Bristol Bay Packing Company in 1916 and converted into a six-masted barquentine and used in the Alaska salmon trade until 1924. She was broken up in a California yard in 1930. There is an illustration of the *City of Sydney* as a six-masted barquetine on page 175 of the book 'Pacific Square-Riggers: Pictorial History of the Great Windships of Yesteryear' by Jim Gibbs. Another illustration appears on page 231 of 'Australian Steamships Past and Present' by Dickson Gregory.

The original engines for the three vessels were built by the Morgan Iron Works of New York and had been designed for J. Roach and Sons by Thomas Main, acting under the guidance of Edward Farron, the superintendent of construction for the Pacific Mail Steamship Company. The vertical compound, surface-condensing engines developed 1,900 indicated horsepower and had cylinders of 88 inches and 51 inches. The air pumps, circulating pumps, feed pumps and the single bilge pump were independent of the main engines. These pumps were worked by a separate pair of engines and were not affected by the racing of the main engines in rough weather. There were six boilers each containing 204 tubes that were built by the Delaware River Iron Works. The *City of San Francisco* achieved a speed of 14 knots on trials with a steam pressure of 80 psi, a vacuum of 28 inches and main engine revolutions of 55 rpm.

In 1893 the Southern Pacific Railroad acquired a controlling interest in the Pacific Mail Steamship Company. In 1916 the Pacific Mail faced rising costs and was restricted from using the Panama Canal. The Southern Pacific Railroad decided to cease all shipping operations and Grace Line acquired most of the company's fleet and Pacific Mail continued operations as a subsidiary of the Grace Line. In 1925 the Dollar family acquired the Pacific Mail name, house flag and goodwill from Grace Line. In 1938 the U.S. Maritime Commission judged the Dollar Line to be unsound and the government assumed control of Dollar Line and renamed the company American President Lines (APL). In 1997 the APL merged with Neptune Orient Lines (NOL) to create one of the world's largest global transportation companies.

PETE RUDDLE, Casa Grande, AZ 85222, USA

FROM THE BOSUN'S LOCKER
John Clarkson

Containers: the early days

In recent months two books have been published in the USA which mark the 50th anniversary of the first shipment of containers by sea in the USA. Having seen one of the books briefly and a review of the other, one gets the impression that the carriage of containers by sea was a US invention. Not so: the first commercial shipments of containers were made in the United Kingdom – from Preston to Larne in Northern Ireland in September 1954. The ship involved was a small Dutch coaster, the *Prior*. She had not been modified or specially constructed to carry containers and on a good day, from memory, she could manage a maximum of 20 twenty-foot containers of which six or seven were carried athwartships on deck. The total tonnage carried was usually in the region of 200 tons – an average of ten tons per container.

Loading and discharging was done using a Scotch derrick – a ladder was put up against each container in turn, a docker went up onto the roof of the container and hooked chains to lugs at each corner of the container. He then came down, or jumped across onto the next container which would be parked alongside, and the container was lifted onboard – no Health and Safety Executive in those days. The same performance was repeated on the ship. It was some years before twist locks, special container cranes and purpose-built spreaders came in. Over the following 15 years or so the business thrived, bigger ships were introduced and more services started to other Irish ports ranging from Londonderry in the north round to Greenore and Dublin in the south. For a time there was a service to Iberia and Sealand had a feeder service to and from Rotterdam. Strikes at big UK ports often resulted in containers arriving on feeders from Rotterdam.

However, these were not the first containers to be shipped through Preston, and more may have gone via railway ports and steamers. Even in pre-war days small wooden containers were carried on Hugh Craig's steamers, such as the *Helen Craig* on the services to and from Belfast. These small containers were designed to carry cotton to Ireland for bleaching and dying and for bringing back the finished products. The other difference with these boxes is that they were intended for rail, rather than road transport.

The Suez crisis in 1956 gave containers a boost. We had several former landing craft running to Ireland carrying ro-ro traffic. When these ships were taken up for government service no suitable replacements were available. The answer was to crane trailers on to British coasters such as *Cliffville* (965/1944), *Loch Linnhe* (766/1928) and *Glenapp Castle* (642/1924). Foreign coasters were also used of which *Mary Robert Muller* (1,598/1952), *Fidentia* (998/1955) and

Prior (499/1951) arriving at Preston with a full deck cargo. Originally owned by A. C. Hoff she ran from Preston until October 1967, changing her name to *Trinitas* in July 1963. *[J. and M. Clarkson collection]*

Kapt. Jan Reinecke (1,489/1950) but despite these being larger their carrying capacity for containers and trailers was still very limited. No doubt some companies changed over to boxes rather than risk their trailers being carried in this way.

Preston was in the forefront of carrying bananas in containers. Geest Line had regular services from Preston and Barry to the West Indies and carried out trials with specially-designed eight-foot containers. The idea worked but never took off and palletisation seemed to suit the trade better.

As the container became a more popular mode of transport on the Irish Sea bigger ships came into service, sailing at scheduled times and Preston, being tidal, lost out to ports such as Heysham, Fleetwood and Liverpool.

Record 34 - more on the *Wollowra*

1/34. On the identification of this ship as *Wollowra*, Ian Farquhar makes the point that the tall funnel she had as *Silvio Spaventa* prevailed

for a time when she was with Adelaide Steam but was later shortened, which might suggest that the first owner put the star on the funnel.

Huntingdon's mainmast

We are grateful to the readers who responded to John B. Hill's query about when and why *Huntingdon* lost her mainmast, including Ian Farquhar, John Goble, Barry Parsons and Tony Smythe.

The mainmast was a characteristic of the New Zealand/Federal fleet's visual identity. However, where the ship had its derricks rigged at pairs of samson posts the mast served little useful purpose. It carried the after steaming light and secured one end of the main aerial, both items capable of being located elsewhere, so its principal advantage was that it showed off the flag wardrobe. This comprised the distinctive house flag of New Zealand Shipping which had to be carefully broken out in its separate constituents when hoisted and the almost universal Blue Ensign flown whenever other ships might be encountered. It was a little vanity that had to be abandoned once the

Hauraki showing the beam added between the forward derrick posts to take a steaming light once her mainmast had been removed. *[Ships in Focus]*

Harrison's *Statesman* anchored at Spithead in 1916 waiting to take six MLs and a cargo of TNT into Portsmouth. *[Collection of World Ship Society Ltd.]*

ravages of rust, the old enemy, passed a certain point. It is interesting to note that the *Hororata* managed her long career without a mainmast, steel being at a premium when she was built in wartime.

In 1965 or 1966 the mainmasts were removed from seven of the eight *Haparangi* class ships: *Cumberland*, *Haparangi*, *Hauraki*, *Hertford*, *Huntingdon*, *Hurunui* and *Sussex*. Only the *Hinakura*'s mainmast survived to go to the breakers with the rest of the ship. The object was to reduce maintenance costs at a time when belt-tightening was advisable, and removal saved the cost of scaling and painting the mast and blacking down the rigging. A light girder was fitted between the tops of the forward pair of derrick posts and the steaming light was mounted on a short stub mast located on the centre line. The original foremast steaming light became the after steaming light. Tony Smythe has seen a photograph of *Hauraki* with a wire strung between her aftermost pair of derrick posts and a halliard hung from it for flying the ensign.

The mainmasts were also removed from the New Zealand Shipping Company's passenger liners *Rangitane*, *Rangitoto* and *Ruahine* during 1965, and a tripod erected at the fore end of the funnel to take the after steaming light. This marked a departure from the company's previous policy of having two masts which had even extended to the addition of a mainmast to the *Remuera*, ex *Parthia*, when this ship was bought from Cunard late in 1961 and refitted the following year.

Photographs in 'Record' 35
1/35. Kevin O'Donoghue identified this ship as *Caprera* (3,447/1902), built by Short Brothers Ltd., Sunderland for the British and Chilean Steamship Co. Ltd. (W. Lowden and Co., managers), Liverpool. In 1911 she was sold to Becchi & Calcagno of Savona and renamed *Amor*. She was torpedoed by *U 66* on 5th June 1917 west of Ireland whilst on a voyage from Galveston to Liverpool. Thanks also to George Robinson for attempting to identify this ship.

2/35. Alan Savory kindly supplied two further illustrations of this wreck, which is identified as *Avaré*, sunk in Hamburg. The full story comes thanks to James Cooper, who tells us that the *Avaré* capsized and sank on 16th June 1922 whilst undocking from Vulkan Werft, the cause being incorrect ballasting, a mistake resulting in 39 deaths. The ship had been built for Norddeutscher Lloyd, Bremen as *Sierra Salvada* (8,227/1913). She was at Rio de Janeiro in August 1914 and was laid up there until 1st June 1917 when seized by the Brazilian government who renamed her *Avaré* and entrusted management to Lloyd Brasileiro. After the mishap at Hamburg *Avaré* was refloated on 7th September 1922 and sold to Viktor Schuppe, Stettin who renamed her *Peer Gynt*. In 1926 she was sold to SITMAR of Genoa who added a second funnel and renamed her *Neptunia* but within a

year she was back in German ownership as Hapag's *Oceana*. In 1935 she was transferred to Deutsche Arbeitsfront G.m.b.H. with Hamburg-Amerika Linie as managers to run 'strength through joy' cruises. December 1939 saw her become an accommodation ship for the Kriegsmarine. In June 1945 she was initially claimed by the British and given the name *Empire Tarne*, but in February 1946 was reallocated to the USSR who used her as the naval depot ship *Sibir* in the Pacific. She was broken up at Vladivostok in 1963.

3/35. Much detective work has been put in by John Chandler, Tony Smith and John B. Hill on this photograph, purporting to show the *Statesman* in November 1915.

In early 1915 the Royal Navy ordered motor launches (MLs) from Elco in the USA. These were to replace requisitioned craft that were not really suitable for the support work for which they were used. The US company supplied the parts, which were fabricated in Canada. Photograph 3/35 shows a merchant ship modified to carry four MLs, one of which is clearly ML 41. All the MLs were shipped across the Atlantic as deck cargo on merchant ships and then fitted out and armed with a three-pounder gun at Portsmouth. ML 41 has no gun and so is clearly being shipped from Canada. Delivery began in October 1915, so the November 1915 date fits well, especially as the MLs were presumably built in numeric order. A dozen MLs were sent out to Egypt, but the first of these did not leave Portsmouth until 13th January 1916. Harrison's four-masted *Statesman* was definitely used in shipping MLs, and Tony Smith kindly lent the accompanying photograph showing her anchored at Spithead in 1916 with a cargo of six MLs protected by wooden palissades. This discounts the theory suggested by one reader that, in view of the 500 plus MLs ordered, it was worth taking the masts out of *Statesman* to expedite shipments. In any case, the ship in photograph 3/35 has a different profile to the Harrison vessel. John Chandler tells us a total of 130 merchant ships were used to carry the MLs, but unfortunately he only knows the names of three others – *Diyatalawa*, *Queensland* and *Daleby*. Identifying the ship in 3/35 still remains a challenge.

4/35. Ben Scholten and John B. Hill had little trouble in identifying this First World War ship as the *Agamemnon* (1,904/1914) of Koninklijke Nederlandsche Stoomboot Maatschappij, Amsterdam. Built by Dunlop, Bremner and Co. at Port Glasgow, whilst new she was the first Dutch ship to transit the Panama Canal, and both readers sent us copies of a photograph showing this event. Ben believes photograph 4/35 was taken just after March 1918 when the British government took her under the right of angary, the claim of a belligerent power to seize the ship of a neutral country for its own use.

In line with maritime law, following the war *Agamemnon* was restored to her Dutch owners and they would have been due payment for her use by Great Britain. She lasted until 8th November 1940 when she sailed from Ridham Dock for the Tyne in ballast and was sunk by air attack near the Swin Light Vessel.

Obituary: Ivor Rooke

The death occurred of Ivor Rooke at his home in Itchenor, West Sussex on 14th November 2006, aged 84 years. Ivor was an avid supporter and regular behind the scenes contributor to this magazine.

Born on 20th May 1922, Ivor was brought up as a child near Hove and encouraged by his father to find an interest or hobby, he commenced recording details of ships and shipping on his way home from school at Shoreham. His meticulous record keeping and sketches of ships, made from the cliffs at Kingsgate near North Foreland in the 1950s, were to later appear in books on coasters and bulk carriers.

His working life was spent with Lloyds Bank, and he saw war service with the Army, serving with the Royal Sussex Regiment, and retained a keen interest in military history.

A favourite holiday of Ivor's was to the continent, to see the ships at Vlissingen, Antwerp and Rotterdam. It was only back in September, with failing health, that his son Michael took him to his favourite spot at Vlissingen for a short break. It is fitting indeed that on what was to be his last day he was still busy compiling the records of ships photographed and seen during that trip.

A specialist in bulk carriers and tramp shipping, Ivor will be sadly missed both by this magazine and all its readers. He leaves a wife Peggy, and two sons Michael and Peter, to whom we extend our sympathy.

1/36. This photo is taken from a postcard which has not been used so we have no date. At a guess the ship is a cross-channel ferry on war service. She certainly has plenty of troops on deck.

2/36. A good clear picture of a clipper-bowed ship, background not recognised but the card was produced in Canada. Could this be one of the C.P.R. *Empress* ships which ran between Canada and Japan?

3/36. This is a photo we would like to use in our publication on Clan Line but we are not certain of the identity of the left hand ship. On the back of the print there is a note *Clan Cameron* but *Cameron* has been deleted and replaced by *Forbes*. The left hand ship is unlikely to be *Clan Forbes* – she had two derrick posts aft of the superstructure and an extra deck above the engine room casing. *Clan Cameron* had a mast at the after end of the superstructure and no extra deck as in this photo. We think this photo was correctly identified in the first place as *Clan Cameron* but maybe a reader can confirm, and identify the damaged ship on the right.

Laurence worked closely with Blue Funnel and Glen Lines and produced this painting in the mid-1960s of one of the handsome Glen Line *Glenalmond*-class ships.

Above: An evocative image of *Peleus* (10,093/1949) and *Clan Kenneth* (7,174/1942) at Glasgow in the 1950s.

Left: A 1950s Clan Line brochure, one of many promotional items produced over the years.

LAURENCE DUNN
A RETROSPECTIVE OF A PROLIFIC TALENT
Peter Newall

On the 30th November 2006, Laurence Dunn, the undisputed doyen of ship lovers around the world passed away peacefully at Gravesend aged 96. His career spanned much of the 20th century and his legacy as a shipping artist and writer was quite remarkable.

Laurence and his wife Jennifer, who is also an accomplished artist and often wrote articles with him.

Born at Llandaff on April 9th 1910, Laurence spent most of his childhood in the Devon port of Brixham. From an early age, he became interested in ships and spent a lot of his time identifying the numerous ships, which called for bunkers. His talent for drawing was soon evident as he made sketches of the ships he saw. These were later transformed into detailed small profile drawings, which became his trademark and led to his employment during the war years producing ship recognition manuals for the Admiralty. He was also a prolific photographer and at thirteen, took his first photograph of a ship.

After formal art training at the Paignton Art College and Central School of Art in London, Laurence's first client was Southern Railway who required profiles of all their ships. This was followed in 1934 by work for Orient Line's new *Orion* and *Orcades*, which were among the finest British liners of the 20th century. He proposed a corn colour hull with green boot topping for these ships, a distinctive colour scheme, which was used for all new Orient liners right up to the *Oriana* of 1960.

In the late 1930s, the first of his extraordinary cutaway drawings appeared. These showed the internal workings of a ship with an accuracy, which has never been surpassed. They were done for a number of shipyards, including Burntisland and Hall, Russell, and well known publications such as Everybody's and the Sphere. However, it was the ones produced in the 1950s and 1960s for the popular boy's comic, the Eagle, which inspired a new generation of ship enthusiasts. Many books followed including his classic Ship Recognition series and "Passenger Liners".

A perfectionist in everything he did, Laurence's eye for detail was legendary and he was engaged by the leading shipping lines of the day to produce paintings of their latest ships. These were used in all kinds of promotional material from brochures to postcards. He also designed stamps and in 1955 produced an ingenious make-your-own press-out model of the new Royal Yacht *Britannia*.

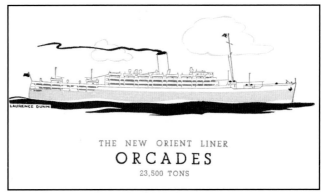

THE NEW ORIENT LINER
ORCADES
23,500 TONS

Orcades with Orient Line's corn-coloured hull.

Laurence Dunn's influence was universal. Unlike many of the marine writers of his generation, who are mainly forgotten, his knowledge lives on in his writings and paintings. It also continues to grow among those of us who learned their trade through his brilliant teaching.

Protea was one of a pair of 307gt steam trawlers built at Aberdeen in 1938 by Hall Russell & Co. Ltd. for Irvin and Johnson Ltd., Cape Town.

1980 set of Fiji stamps showing ships which served the islands. Laurence did the entire design, including the lettering.

July 1931, the Watts, Watts tramps, *Medmenham* (3,474/1904/) and *Wooburn* (3,930/1905) seen laid up at Malpas in the River Fal, Cornwall. They were both demolished in 1933.

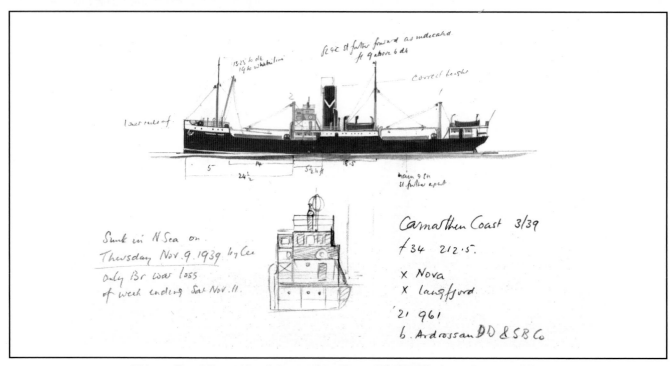

This profile of Coast Lines' *Carmarthen Coast* (961/1921) shows how carefully
Laurence analysed ships.

UNDER THE STAR AND CRESCENT:
BRITISH-BUILT SHIPS OWNED IN PAKISTAN - Part 3
Peter Myers

IMTIAZBAKSH (right)
William Pickersgill and Sons Ltd.,
Sunderland; 1956, 6,247gt, 457 feet
T. 3-cyl. and low-pressure turbine with
double reduction gearing and hydraulic
coupling by North Eastern Marine
Engineering Co. (1938) Ltd.
A year after the purchase of the *Ramsay*
from the Bolton Steam Shipping Co. Ltd.,
London, United Oriental bought the five-
year-old *Reynolds* from the same company
in 1961 and renamed her *Imtiazbaksh*.
Her propulsion machinery complemented
that of the company's *Yousuf Baksh*. Her
career ended 15 years later when she
arrived at Karachi in May 1976 for
breaking up. *[Fotoship/Peter Newall*
collection]

SAFINA-E-ISMAIL (above)
William Pickersgill and Sons Ltd.,
Sunderland; 1958, 5,902gt, 465 feet
4-cyl. Doxford-type oil engine by North
Eastern Marine Engineering Co. Ltd.,
Wallsend-on-Tyne.
The *Safina-e-Ismail* was originally the

Essex Trader of the Trader Navigation Co.
Ltd., London, and was bought by the Pan-
Islamic Steamship Co. Ltd. in 1963. She
traded for her Karachi owners for a
remarkable 24 years before she arrived at
Gadani Beach in December 1987 to be
broken up. The Pan-Islamic came under

the control of the Pakistan Government in
1974, but was returned to the private
sector in 1980 because of the Saudi
Arabian interests in the company, and was
run by Mr. A.D. Ahmed. *[J. and M.*
Clarkson collection]

223

RUPSA

Bartram and Sons Ltd., Sunderland; 1958, 8,525gt, 477 feet
6-cyl. Doxford-type oil engine by William Doxford and Sons (Engineers) Ltd., Sunderland.

The *Rupsa* was formerly the *La Falda* (top) of Buries Markes Ltd., London, and had been launched as the *Montcalm*. She was the last of the company's cargo ships to be built with engines amidships, because the *La Marea*, which was completed by the same yard three months later, set the trend for all the firm's subsequent ships which had engines and superstructure aft. The *La Falda* became the *Rupsa* (middle right) after the National Shipping Corporation of Karachi bought her in 1964. In August 1970 a national dock strike in Britain resulted in the *Rupsa*'s jute consignment for Dundee being discharged at Antwerp where it remained until the strike was over. The Panamanian cargo ship *Sparta* (1,743/1956) was chartered to bring the 1,375 tons of jute bales and gunnies to Dundee. On 6th November 1976 the *Rupsa* was in collision with the *Agelos Raphael* (13,359/1964) while on passage from Karachi to Baltimore. She was declared a constructive loss and offered for sale 'as is', and in 1977 was bought by Louiseville General Enterprises Inc. and refitted. A year later she passed to La Compagnie de Navigation Louiseville and was renamed *Caron P.E.* under the Liberian flag. The Maldives Shipping Co. Ltd. bought her in 1980 and she was renamed *Maldive Image* under the Maldives flag. On 6th July 1982 she had the misfortune to run aground off Mukalla, South Yemen, during heavy weather while inbound with a cargo of bagged rice from Bangkok. She was abandoned as a constructive total loss for the second time in her career. *[J. and M. Clarkson collection]*

KAROTUA and SWAT

Barclay Curle and Co. Ltd., Whiteinch, Glasgow; 1958, 8,301gt, 487 feet

6-cyl. Doxford-type oil engine by Barclay Curle and Co. Ltd., Whiteinch, Glasgow. An important purchase by the National Shipping Corporation in 1967 were the sister ships *Weybridge* (below) and *Wimbledon* from Watts, Watts and Co. Ltd. of London, which were renamed *Karotua* (opposite top right) and *Swat* (opposite middle right) respectively. The pair had attracted widespread attention when completed in 1958 because of the highly individual nature of their design, which stemmed from the company's chairman,

Edmund H. Watts. Both ships' hull lines were largely the result of Edmund Watts's study of fish, as were the fins aft, just forward of the propeller. The very pronounced hull knuckles forward and aft helped seakindliness by damping out pitching movement. All the London company's ships had a very high standard of accommodation, and in the *Weybridge* and *Wimbledon* the single cabins for the crew extended the length of the midship structure and which opened out on to long galleries just inside the hull and were

furnished with tables and easy chairs. The crew also had a place set aside for deck tennis, cafeteria messing and a swimming pool right forward. The ships' 16 derricks served six holds, of which the sixth was aft of the machinery space. The *Wimbledon* was chartered by the Port Line Ltd. between 1960-65 and renamed *Port Wimbledon,* while the *Weybridge* was chartered by Lamport and Holt in 1964 and renamed *Rossetti* before reverting to *Weybridge* at the end of the charter. In March 1971, during the mounting tension in East Pakistan, the *Swat* arrived at Chittagong with munitions and equipment for the Pakistani armed forces. Bengali dock workers refused to co-operate with the army in unloading the ship and she remained idle for more than two weeks. The army then went ahead and unloaded the *Swat*, a move which provoked widespread protests in Chittagong and resulted in a violent crackdown by the army. Both the *Karotua* and the *Swat* were sold to Pakistani shipbreakers and broken up at Gadani Beach in 1982. *[Weybridge: John G. Callis/J. and M. Clarkson, Karotua and Swat: Ships in Focus]*

SIPSAH (below)
William Gray and Co. Ltd, West Hartlepool; 1959, 5,577gt, 463 feet Two steam turbines double-reduction geared to a single shaft by Central Marine Engine Works, West Hartlepool.
The *Sipsah* was originally the *Mary Holt* of the Guinea Gulf Line Ltd., Liverpool, and traded to West Africa. My uncle, the late Captain Hubert Tennant, was master of the *Mary Holt* in the early 1960s. When the Guinea Gulf Line was purchased by Liner Holdings, the parent company of Elder Dempster Lines, in 1965, the *Mary*

Holt was one of four ships acquired in the deal, but the turbine steamers could not be easily integrated into Elder Dempster's fleet of motor ships. All four ships were sold to other owners as soon as possible, although the *Mary Holt* made one round voyage to West Africa under Elder Dempster management before she was acquired by the National Shipping Corporation, Karachi, in

September 1965. During the Indo-Pakistan War of December 1971, the *Sipsah* evaded Indian air and naval patrols to bring Chinese arms to Karachi. Her ten-year trading career under the Pakistan flag ended when she was sold for demolition at Gadani Beach in November 1975. *[Airfoto of Malacca/J. and M. Clarkson collection]*

JHELUM

Hawthorn Leslie (Shipbuilders) Ltd.,
Hebburn; 1960, 8,282gt, 466 feet
5-cyl. Doxford-type diesel by Hawthorn
Leslie (Shipbuilders) Ltd., Hebburn.

The Moor Line Ltd., managed by Walter
Runciman and Co. Ltd., had a series of six
tramps built on the Tyne between 1956 and
1961, named *Glenmoor, Hazelmoor,*
Innesmoor, Jedmoor, Kirriemoor (above)
and *Linkmoor.* The *Jedmoor* and the
Kirriemoor were sold to the newly created
National Shipping Corporation of Pakistan
in 1964 after comparatively short trading
careers with Runciman, being renamed
Ravi (middle right) and *Jhelum* (bottom
right) respectively, these being two of the
five rivers which flow through the Punjab.
Not long after her purchase, the *Jhelum*
was involved in a collision with the
Danish ship *Cynthia* in the Thames on 1st
January 1965. The distinctive feature of
the *Jedmoor* and *Kirriemoor*, which were
of the open shelter deck type, was the long
superstructure. There were six holds of
which that served by number 3 hatch was
aft of the bridge, but being flanked by
accommodation was trunked to a higher
level. The ships had a 30-ton jumbo
derrick, as well as ten others of five- to 10-
tons capacity. The 'tween deck spaces and
all holds were fitted for the shipment of
grain cargoes, an important consideration
for her Pakistani owners. Both sisters' oil
engines were fitted to burn heavy fuel oil
and gave a service speed of 14.5 knots.
Just before the outbreak of the Indo-
Pakistan War in December 1971, three
destroyers of the Pakistan Navy, the
Jahangir, Khaibar and the *Tippu Sultan,*
were sent to locate the *Jhelum* in the
Arabian Sea and escort her to the safety of
Karachi. The *Jhelum*'s owners became the

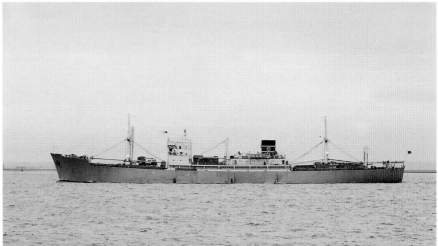

Pakistan Shipping Corporation in 1974 and
then the Pakistan National Shipping
Corporation in 1979. She continued
trading until laid-up at Karachi in March
1983 and was sold for demolition to

Pakistani shipbreakers at the end of that
year. Her sister-ship *Ravi* had been broken
up at Gadani Beach a year earlier. *[Top*
and middle: J. and M. Clarkson, Bottom:
Ships in Focus]

226

SAFINA-E-HAIDER
Fairfield Shipbuilding and Engineering Co. Ltd., Govan, Glasgow; 1963, 9,210gt, 465 feet
6-cyl. Sulzer-type oil engine by Fairfield-Rowan Ltd., Glasgow.

The *Safina-e-Haider* was built as the *Lancashire* (above) for Bibby Brothers and Co. Ltd. of Liverpool, and was the last Bibby ship designed for the company's old-established route to Burma. She made her maiden voyage to Rangoon in 1964, but afterwards was placed on the charter market. The *Lancashire* was sold in 1970 to Pargola (Shipping) Ltd. of London, who quickly resold her to the Pan-Islamic Steamship Co. Ltd. of Karachi. The author saw the *Safina-e-Haider* (below) in February 1983 at Hong Kong, where she had arrived from Japan on her owners' Far East-Red Sea/Eastern Mediterranean service. She was advertised as making subsequent calls at Colombo, Jeddah, Port Said, Alexandria, Limassol, Beirut and Lattakia. The company's *Safina-e-Rehmat* (8,595/1958) was scheduled to follow on the same service a month later. It was encouraging to see a 20-year-old ship still able to earn a living in the liner trades, and the *Safina-e-Haider* continued trading for another ten years for Pan-Islamic until sold in 1993 for demolition at Gadani Beach. The Pan-Islamic company no longer owns ships, but still exists, on paper, and continues to be quoted on the Karachi Stock Exchange. *[Top: J. and M. Clarkson, bottom: Ships in Focus]*

OCEAN ENDEAVOUR (right)
*Lithgows Ltd., Port Glasgow; 1965,
11,950gt, 527 feet*
*6-cyl. Sulzer-type oil engine by Fairfield-
Rowan Ltd., Glasgow.*
The *Ocean Endeavour* was one of the first
bulk carriers owned in Pakistan, having
been built as the *Cape Rodney* for the Lyle
Shipping Co. Ltd. of Glasgow. She was
bought by the Trans-Oceanic Steamship
Co. Ltd., Karachi, in 1971 and just three
years later was taken over by the Pakistan
Shipping Corporation. The *Ocean
Endeavour* was broken up at Gadani
Beach in 1984. *[J. and M. Clarkson
collection]*

PUSSUR (above)
*Bartram and Sons Ltd., Sunderland;
1965, 6,249gt, 498 feet*
*6-cyl. Sulzer-type diesel by George Clark
and North Eastern Marine Ltd., Wallsend-
on-Tyne.*
The *Pussur* was launched as *Teesta* for the
National Shipping Corporation, but her
name was changed to *Pussur* after the river
which flows through East Pakistan (now
Bangladesh) and on which the important
jute-loading port of Chalna stands. The
Pussur, which had refrigerated cargo
space, was sometimes employed on her
owners' liner service from Karachi to the
U.K., calling at Avonmouth and Liverpool.
She was broken up at Gadani Beach in
1984. *[Peter Newall collection]*

OCEAN ENDURANCE (opposite top)
*Bartram and Sons Ltd., Sunderland; 1966,
7,795gt, 502 feet*
*6-cyl. Sulzer-type oil engine by Hawthorn,
Leslie (Engineers) Ltd., Hebburn.*

The *Ocean Endurance* was built for the
Trans-Oceanic Steamship Co. Ltd.,
Karachi, as a combination passenger/cargo
ship. She had air-conditioned cabin
accommodation for 25 first-class
passengers and could accommodate 250
economy-class passengers in her 'tween
decks and was particularly suited for
trading between the west and east wings of
Pakistan. The *Ocean Endurance* and
Trans-Oceanic's other two ships, the bulk
carrier *Ocean Endeavour* and the SD14
type cargo ship *Ocean Envoy,* were taken
over by the Pakistan Shipping Corporation
in 1974. The *Ocean Endurance* sometimes returned to British waters and in
August 1973 she could be found in the
Brocklebank Dock, Liverpool. Her trading
career ended more than 10 years later
when she arrived at Karachi in April 1984
before proceeding along the coast to be
broken up at Gadani Beach. *[Peter
Newall collection]*

OHRMAZD (opposite bottom)
*Burntisland Shipbuilding Co. Ltd.,
Burntisland; 1968, 11,046gt, 515 feet*
*6-cyl. Sulzer oil engine by George Clark
and North Eastern Marine Ltd.,
Sunderland.*
Like the *Ocean Endurance*, the *Ohrmazd*
was a combined passenger/cargo ship and
had accommodation for 276 passengers,
and was the first newbuilding for her
owners, the East and West Steamship Co.
(1961), whose partnership had been recon-
stituted in that year. The *Ohrmazd*'s
construction was financed by the British
Government as part of its overseas aid to
Pakistan, but her building was bedevilled
by disputes over the specifications and
contract terms between the Burntisland yard
and the Karachi shipowners. These led to
serious delays in her completion and
resulted in the yard suffering heavy
financial penalties, which it could ill-afford.
The *Ohrmazd* was completed in November
1968, but the damage had been done and

the Fife yard went into liquidation the following month. On her maiden voyage the *Ohrmazd* was strikebound at Baltimore for several months by a dispute involving longshoremen. The *Ohrmazd* plied between West and East Pakistan, a trade which was seriously disrupted by the civil war in East Pakistan in 1971 and which culminated in independence for Bangladesh at the end of that year. Her owners were nationalised in 1974, and their two ships, *Ohrmazd* and *Rustom* (the 1953-built former *Santa Teresa* of Hamburg Sud-Amerika Line), were taken over by the Pakistan Shipping Corporation. The *Ohrmazd* arrived for demolition at Gadani Beach on 6th July 1994. *[Peter Newall collection]*

BRITISH YARD, GREEK TRAMP - REVISITED
Paul Boot

It is exactly eight years since 'British Yard, Greek Tramp' appeared, way back in 'Record 8', and we are pleased to return to this fascinating and often confusingly complex subject.

With many of the Greek companies having offices in London, it is not surprising that British shipyards were favoured with orders for new ships after the war. In his monumental, five volume work 'Kings of the Oceans', George Foustanos provides a full account of all new ships built for Greek principals between 1948 and 1980 and the dominance of British builders for much of this period is evident. *Mary* (5,685/1949), built by William Gray for N. G. Livanos, was the first of many ships for Greek owners and this yard would deliver a further 19 tramps, largely to Livanos and Michalinos, before its closure in 1962. Doxford's output was equally impressive with no fewer than 26 vessels, the last of which could perhaps be more accurately described as cargo liners rather than tramps. Rivalling even this, with 50 ships delivered to Greek principals, was the combined production of the SD14 type by the Austin and Pickersgill, and Bartram yards,

recapturing a market that had during the early 1960s largely been lost to Japanese and other foreign builders.

In total well over 150 dry-cargo ships were delivered, but not all flew the Greek flag. Some operators, such as Lykiardopulo and Stravros Livanos, chose to establish a British subsidiary until the commercial advantages of doing so had rapidly evaporated during the mid 1950s. More common though was the practice of placing ships under a flag of convenience, usually registered to a single-ship company whose office was often located in a country other than that indicated by the port of registry. It is indeed often difficult to differentiate between the true owners and managers, although funnel colours are generally a reliable guide, and in some instances even 'Lloyd's Confidential Index' cautiously lists the operator as no more than 'agents for' the owning companies.

To supplement the selection of photographs, details of all the ships ordered from British shipyards by the operators featured in this and the previous portfolio are listed below with principal dimensions and machinery details.

		Builders	Year	Gross Tons	Length x breadth (feet)	Main engine type and builders	Renamed / Notes
P.G. CALLIMANOPULOS (Hellenic Lines Limited)							
HELLENIC GLORY	●	Hamilton	56	7,510	486x64	6-cyl Doxford oil engine by Fairfield, Glasgow	
HELLENIC TORCH		Hamilton	56	7,510	486x54	6-cyl Doxford oil engine by Fairfield, Glasgow	
A. J. & D. J. CHANDRIS							
DONA EDIE	◆	Doxford (2)	57	9,746	509x67	4-cyl oil engine by builders	ISOBEL
DONA KATERINA	◆	Doxford (2)	57	9,746	509x67	4-cyl oil engine by builders	
DONA MARGARITA	◆●	Doxford (1)	56	8,716	483x62	4-cyl oil engine by builders	MARIRITA
DONA OURANIA		Doxford (1)	56	8,716	483x62	4-cyl oil engine by builders	
MISS CHANDRIS	◆	Doxford (2)	59	9,855	509X67	6-cyl oil engine by builders	GENIE
COULOUTHROS Ltd.							
AEGEAN ISLAND		Burntisland	57	8,184	469x60	7-cyl B&W oil engine by J.G. Kincaid, Greenock	[PARNASSOS] ●
MICHAEL C.		Swan	56	7,905	466x60	4-cyl Doxford oil engine by builders	
POLYXENE C	●	Swan	57	9,166	501x64	5-cyl Doxford oil engine by builders	
S. G. EMBIRICOS Ltd.							
NICOLAOS S EMBIRICOS		Cam. Laird	58	6,279	470X62	4-cyl Doxford oil engine by North East Marine Engineering Co. Ltd., Wallsend	
STAMATIOS G EMBIRICOS	◆●	Doxford (2)	56	8,878	486x62	4-cyl oil engine by builders	
managed for **Z.L. & G.L. Cambanis**							
DORIEFS	●	Cam. Laird	58	6,331	481x63	7-cyl oil engine by Sulzer Bros., Winterthur	
DORIS	◆	Cam. Laird	54	6,042	470x62	4-cyl oil engine by Sulzer Bros., Winterthur	[IRIS] ●
D.J. FAFALIOS							
FAETHON		Doxford (3)	71	11,502	540x70	7-cyl Sulzer oil engine by G. Clark & N.E.M. Ltd. Wallsend	
FEAX		Doxford (3)	70	11,489	540x70	7-cyl Sulzer oil engine by G. Clark & N.E.M. Ltd. Wallsend	
FINIX	●	Doxford (3)	69	11,489	540x70	7-cyl Sulzer oil engine by G. Clark & N.E.M. Ltd. Wallsend	
STAMOS	◆	Short	56	8,789	491x61	7-cyl B&W oil engine by J.G. Kincaid, Greenock	
FAROS SHIPPING Co. Ltd. (Michael M. Xylas)							
ALEXANDROS		Readhead	59	9,735	499x63	6-cyl oil engine by Sulzer Bros., Winterthur	
ANAX		Readhead	55	8,332	473x61	T 3-cyl with low pressure turbine by builder	
APOLLON		Readhead	57	9,451	499x63	6-cyl oil engine by Sulzer Bros., Winterthur	
ATLAS	●	Readhead	58	9,724	499x63	6-cyl oil engine by Sulzer Bros., Winterthur	

		Builders	Year	Gross Tons	Length x breadth (feet)	Main engine type and builders	Renamed / Notes

N.G. LIVANOS *(This title embraces a number of management and ownership arrangements under the 'blue L' Livanos funnel colours)*

		Builders	Year	Gross Tons	Length x breadth	Main engine type and builders	Renamed / Notes
ALIKI LIVANOS		Gray	53	7,409	458x58	T 3-cyl with low pressure turbine by Central Marine Eng. Works, Hartlepool	TARPON BAY
ALIKI LIVANOS		Doxford (2)	65	10,865	540x70	6-cyl oil engine by builders	TARPON SILVER
EVGENIA		Gray	52	7,404	458x58	T 3-cyl with low pressure turbine by Central Marine Eng. Works, Hartlepool	
GEORGIOS	◆	Gray	51	5,739	458x58	T 3-cyl with low pressure turbine by Central Marine Eng. Works, Hartlepool	
KATHERINE		Doxford (2)	64	10,864	540x70	6-cyl oil engine by builders	NEPHELE
LUCY	◆	Gray	57	7,568	457x58	T 3-cyl with low pressure turbine by Central Marine Eng. Works, Hartlepool *Re-engined 1961 with 3-cyl Doxford oil engine*	
MARY		Gray	49	5,685	458x58	T 3-cyl with low pressure turbine by Central Marine Eng. Works, Hartlepool	
N G LIVANOS		Doxford (3)	67	11,025	540x70	6-cyl oil engine by builders	
PEARL BEACH		Gray	58	8,465	478x62	4-cyl oil engine by Wm. Doxford, Sunderland	TARPON BEACH
PEARL CLIPPER		Doxford (2)	60	8,742	486x62	4-cyl oil engine by Wm. Doxford, Sunderland	TARPON CLIPPER
PEARL CREEK	◆●	Gray	58	8,466	478x62	4-cyl Doxford oil engine by Hawthorn Leslie Ltd., Newcastle	LEODAMAS
PEARL HAVEN	◆	Gray	60	8,461	478x62	4-cyl Doxford oil engine by North East Marine Engineering, Wallsend	THETIS
PEARL ISLAND		Doxford (2)	64	10,865	540x70	6-cyl oil engine by builders	
PEARL MERCHANT		Doxford (2)	63	10,867	540x70	6-cyl oil engine by builders	
PEARL SEA		Gray	57	7,977	470x60	4-cyl Doxford oil engine by Hawthorn Leslie Ltd., Newcastle	TARPON SEA
PEARL STONE		Gray	56	8,000	470x60	6-cyl B&W oil engine by J.G. Kincaid, Greenock	TARPON SURF
PEARL TRADER		Doxford (2)	62	10,122	509x67	4-cyl oil engine by builder	

STAVROS LIVANOS

		Builders	Year	Gross Tons	Length x breadth	Main engine type and builders	Renamed / Notes
ATLANTIC COUNTESS		Gray	54	9,833	508x63	Three steam turbines by Parsons, Wallsend	
ATLANTIC EMPRESS	◆	Gray	49	7,527	500x63	4-cyl Doxford oil engine by Hawthorn, Leslie Newcastle	

Trent Maritime Co. Ltd.

		Builders	Year	Gross Tons	Length x breadth	Main engine type and builders	Renamed / Notes
DUKE OF ATHENS [*]		Furness	62	10,815	518x66	5-cyl Doxford oil engine by Hawthorn, Leslie Ltd., Newcastle	ATLANTIC FREEDOM
DUKE OF MISTRA [*]		Furness	60	10,799	518x66	5-cyl Doxford oil engine by Hawthorn, Leslie Ltd., Newcastle	ATLANTIC FURY ●
DUKE OF SPARTA [*]		Furness	59	10,823	518x66	5-cyl Doxford oil engine by Marinens Hovedverft, Horten	ATLANTIC FALCON

LYKIARDOPULO & Co. Ltd.

		Builders	Year	Gross Tons	Length x breadth	Main engine type and builders	Renamed / Notes
ARIADNE		A & P	69	9,38	463x67	5-cyl Sulzer oil engine byG. Clark & N.E.M. Ltd. Wallsend	SD14
DAPHNE	◆	Gray	54	5,779	458x58	T 3-cyl by Central Marine Eng. Works, Hartlepool	
NICOLAOS D.L.		A & P	69	9,038	463x67	5-cyl Sulzer oil engine by Vickers Ltd., Barrow-in-Furness	SD14
NYMPHE	◆	Furness	54	5,653	467x59	4-cyl oil engine by North East Marine Eng.	

Drake Shipping Co. Ltd.

		Builders	Year	Gross Tons	Length x breadth	Main engine type and builders	Renamed / Notes
MERCHANT DUKE [*]		Gray	51	5,891	458x58	T 3-cyl by Central Marine Eng. Works, Hartlepool	
MERCHANT ROYAL [*]		Blythswood	57	9,722	502x63	5-cyl Doxford oil engine by D. Rowan, Glasgow	DIONE

LYRAS Bros. Ltd.

		Builders	Year	Gross Tons	Length x breadth	Main engine type and builders	Renamed / Notes
IASON		Doxford (3)	70	11,489	540x70	7-cyl Sulzer oil engine by G. Clark & N.E.M. Ltd, Wallsend	
IKTINOS		Doxford (3)	69	11,489	540x70	7-cyl Sulzer oil engine by G. Clark & N.E.M. Ltd, Sunderland	
ION		Doxford (3)	71	11,506	540x70	7-cyl Sulzer oil engine by G. Clark & N.E.M. Ltd, Sunderland	
PINDAR	◆	Short	54	6,129	485x61	8-cyl oil engine by Sulzer Bros., Winterthur	VASSILAKIS

MICHALINOS & Co. Ltd.

		Builders	Year	Gross Tons	Length x breadth	Main engine type and builders	Renamed / Notes
APPLEDORE [*]		Gray	53	5,842	458X58	T 3-cyl with low pressure turbine by Central Marine Eng. Works, Hartlepool	
CASTLEDORE [*]	●	Gray	56	7,952	456x60	T 3-cyl with low pressure turbine by Central Marine Eng. Works, Hartlepool	
GEORGIDORE [*]		Readhead	54	8,063	458x59	T 3-cyl with low pressure turbine by builders	
LORADORE [*]		Gray	58	8,077	456x60	4-cyl Doxford oil engine by North East Marine Engineering, Wallsend	[THOMAS A.] ●
RIVERDORE [*]		Gray	59	8,080	456x60	5-cyl Doxford oil engine by Hawthorn Leslie Ltd., Newcastle	
STRATIDORE [*]		Gray	49	4,786	432x56	T 3-cyl by Central Marine Eng. Works, Hartlepool	

		Builders	Year	Gross Tons	Length x breadth (feet)	Main engine type and builders	Renamed / Notes
GEORGE NICOLAU Ltd.							
MASTER GEORGE		Readhead	55	7,471	473x61	T 3-cyl with low pressure turbine by builder	
POLI		Denny	54	8,825	492x63	Three steam turbines by builder	
Ships Finance and Management Co. Ltd.							
LORD BYRON [*]		Scotts	57	9,364	501X63	5-cyl Doxford oil engine by builder	
LORD CODRINGTON [*]		Scotts	58	9,364	501X63	5-cyl Doxford oil engine by builder	
LORD GLADSTONE [*]	●	Scotts	59	11,229	530x67	6-cyl Doxford oil engine by builder	N. ZOGRAFIA
NOMIKOS (LONDON) Ltd.							
KING AEGUS		Blyth	56	8,429	486x61	4-cyl Doxford oil engine by North East Marine Engineering Co. Ltd., Wallsend	
KING THESEUS [*]	●	Blyth	57	9,153	493x63	4-cyl Doxford oil engine by North East Marine Engineering Co. Ltd., Wallsend	
DIAMANTIS PATERAS Ltd.							
DIAMANTIS PATERAS	◆	Readhead	55	6,110	460x59	T 3-cyl with low pressure turbine, by builder	KYVERNITIS
PHOCEAN SHIP AGENCY Ltd. *(Michael N. Eustathiou)*							
MANES		Burntisland	55	8,526	468x62	7-cyl oil engine by Sulzer Bros., Winterthur	
MARGO	●	Burntisland	62	8,951	483x62	5-cyl oil engine by A/B Gotavarken, Gothenburg	
MARIETTA		Burntisland	61	9,221	483x62	5-cyl oil engine by A/B Gotavarken, Gothenburg	MARIETTA E.
MASTER NICOS		Burntisland	53	8,453	468x62	6-cyl oil engine by Sulzer Bros., Winterthur	
RETHYMNIS & KULUKUNDIS Ltd.							
AGHIA MARINA		Doxford (1)	54	6,498	484x62	4-cyl oil engine by builder	
AGHIOS NICOLAOS	●	Doxford (1)	55	6,548	484x62	4-cyl oil engine by builder	
AGHIOS SPYRIDON	◆	Doxford (2)	57	9,921	509x67	4-cyl oil engine by builder	
MARIGO R	●	Doxford (3)	69	10,840	523x70	6-cyl oil engine by Burmeister & Wain, Copenhagen	
PEGASUS	●	Furness	57	10,446	518x66	5-cyl Doxford oil engine by North East Marine Engineering Co. Ltd., Wallsend	
PROCYON		Furness	58	10,414	518x66	5-cyl Doxford oil engine by North East Marine Engineering Co. Ltd., Wallsend	
VASILIOS R	●	A & P	62	10,741	526x68	7-cyl Sulzer by K.M. 'De Scheldt', Flushing	
YANNIS	●	Doxford (2)	63	11,195	539x70	6-cyl oil engine by builder	

Builders	A & P	Austin and Pickersgill Ltd., Sunderland [46]
	Bartram	Bartram and Sons, Ltd. South Dock Sunderland [17]
	Blyth	Blyth Dry Docks and Shipbuilding Co. Ltd., Blyth [2]
	Blythswood	Blythswood Shipbuilding Co. Ltd., Glasgow [5]
	Burntisland	Burntisland Shipbuilding Co. Ltd., Burntisland [9]
	Cam. Laird	Cammell, Laird and Co. (Shipbuilders and Engineers) Ltd., Birkenhead [3]
	Denny	William Denny and Sons Ltd., Dumbarton [3]
	Doxford (1)	William Doxford and Sons Ltd., Sunderland [4]
	Doxford (2)	William Doxford and Sons (Shipbuilders) Ltd., Sunderland [12]
	Doxford (3)	Doxford and Sunderland Shipbulding and Engineering Ltd., Sunderland - Pallion yard [10]
	Furness	Furness Shipbuilding Co. Ltd., Haverton Hill-on-Tees [6]
	Gray	William. Gray and Co., West Hartlepool [20]
	Hamilton	William Hamilton and Co. Ltd., Port Glasgow [2]
	Readhead	John Readhead and Sons Ltd., South Shields, Co. Durham [7]
	Scotts	Scotts' Shipbuilding and Engineering Co. Ltd., Greenock [3]
	Short	Short Brothers Ltd., Sunderland [5]
	Swan	Swan Hunter and Wigham Richardson Ltd, Neptune Works, Newcastle-upon-Tyne [7]

The total number of dry-cargo ships built by each yard for all Greek owners, including those not listed above, is shown in [brackets]

Notes	[*]	*after a ships name indicates that it sailed under the British flag (initially or wholly)*
	◆	*Ship illustrated in Record 8*
	●	*Ship illustrated in Record 36*
	Renamed	*Indicates a renaming by the same owners/managers.*

An italicised name in [brackets] indicates that the ship is illustrated under this name following a sale to new owners.

SD14 indicates a ship of the standard SD14 design

AGHIOS NICOLAOS (above)
The success of Doxford's Economy Ship design had done much to promote the motor engine to tramp ship owners and soon led to the introduction of the larger and more powerful 'Improved Series' whose design was credited to Captain Nicholas Rethymnis. The first ship, *Kassos* (5,215/1939), entered the fleet of Rethymnis and Kulukundis Ltd. in 1939 and Minas Rethymnis returned to the yard after the war with orders for three very similar, but again larger, ships. Although composite superstructures were by now finding acceptance, these retained the original 'split' layout still favoured by these

owners. *Aghios Nicolaos* was launched in October 1954 and entered service the following February registered to Porto Blanco Compania Naviera S.A. under the Panamanian flag. She is seen here passing Tilbury in September 1970 shortly before her sale following which she took a succession of names: *Rodon, Aktis, S.B. Bakare, Chief S.B.Bakare* and finally *Antagoras* as which she ended her career in May 1978, driven aground near Cotonu after a major engine room fire. [*George Gould/World Ship Society Ltd*]

STAMATIOS G. EMBIRICOS (below)
Using the same basic hull-form,

Doxford produced a decidedly contemporary arrangement for less conservative owners. S. G. Embiricos's self named ship was the forerunner of many similar vessels built over the next ten years and can be seen to have more than a passing resemblance to the series subsequently built for Bank Line. *Stamatios G. Embiricos* was illustrated in 'Record 8' in mourning colours, but in this July 1981 view at Rotterdam is resplendent in the company's usual livery. Just months later, however, she was laid up and ultimately despatched to the breakers as *Sword* in 1985. [*David Salisbury*]

DONA MARGARITA (above)
Chandris had five ships built by Doxford between 1956 and 1959. *Dona Margarita,* the first of these, had the same principal dimensions as *Stamatios G. Embiricos* but differed in having neither a raised forecastle nor deck winch-houses. She would spend her whole career with Chandris, for a short period as *Maririta*, and gave them 25 year's service, ending her days at Bombay in June 1981. *[Roy Kittle]*

YANNIS (middle)
Rethymnis placed another order with Doxford in 1962 and took delivery of *Yannis* the following year. Their 'standard' tramp design had grown somewhat over the intervening years with the hull now over 50 feet longer, giving a fifty percent increase in deadweight; and with a six-cylinder engine of more than double the power. Like *Aghios Nicolaos* she sported the colours of Minas Rethymnis and his associates, though surprisingly *Yannis* was managed by Chandris. As the trade for conventional cargo ships declined, particularly for a vessel of this size, she was laid up at Piraeus in 1982 and despatched to breakers in Hong Kong three years later. *[David Salisbury]*

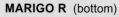

MARIGO R (bottom)
Doxford decided that there was still a market for conventional, geared, cargo ships and produced a revised layout with the engines and superstructure moved towards the stern.

Although the hull now had only straight line sheer, the design was well styled as Rethymnis' *Marigo R,* displaying the charter colours of Deutsche-Afrika Line, clearly shows. *[David Salisbury]*

FINIX (opposite top)
Eight further orders followed from Greek customers, three from D. J. Fafalios. But Doxford, struggling to find orders for their new J-type engine, would not have welcomed this owner's requirement for Sulzer engines which, as they held no license to manufacture, were built on Tyneside. The large raised poop of these later ships is prominent in this stern view of *Finix* sailing from Rotterdam in 1976. *[Paul Boot]*

VASILIOS R (right)

Austin and Pickersgill would construct a considerable number of SD14s for Greek owners but prior to this Rethymnis was the only one to place an order with them. Slightly smaller than *Yannis*, the six hatches and large bipod masts give *Vasilios R* the impression of being a larger ship. Despite her modern appearance, tradition lingered on with a varnished hardwood-fronted bridge-island. In 1977 she became *Ilios* and later *Angeliki S*, with breakers at Kaohsiung taking her in 1987. *[David Salisbury]*

ASTYANAX (below)

During the 1950s Bartram and Sons received a succession of orders for the San Francisco-based Hermes Steamship Agency operated by Andreas Cosmas. Completed in 1956, *Maria C* was the last of their ships to include the family initial in the name and in 1959 she was renamed *Maria K*.

Sold in 1967, she is seen here in March 1973 as *Astyanax* running for one of the smaller Lemos family concerns, Lemos Maritime Co. Ltd., and seemingly not in the best of mechanical order. Having spent the first half of 1976 anchored off at Apapa waiting to

discharge her cargo of cement, her machinery would soon after bring about her demise. Badly damaged by the ensuing fire at Abidjan, she was towed out and scuttled away from the port on Christmas Eve. *[David Salisbury]*

PEARL CREEK (above)
N. G. Livanos remained firmly wedded to the traditional British tramp ship design until the late 1950s, favouring William Gray's yard with a succession of orders. *Lucy* (7,568/1957), the fifth of these ten ships, was the last of the triple-expansion powered tramps and the rest of the series were all fitted with oil engines; as indeed was *Lucy* after just four years' service. *Pearl Creek* was the penultimate example of his Gray-built ships and was renamed *Leodamas* in 1974. Sold in 1978 to other Greek owners, the following year she was badly damaged after grounding and was scrapped in Pakistan. *[Paul Boot]*

CASTLEDORE (middle)
Michalinos Brothers, eager to have a British registered company, had bought the Cardiff tramping concern Maritime Shipping and Trading Co. Ltd. in 1942. They were, like Livanos, traditional ship owners and went to Grays for all but one of their six new ships. *Castledore,* with her modern and stylish superstructure, would easily pass as a contemporary motor-ship were it not for the plume of steam rising skywards. The funnel markings in this April 1970 photograph at Birkenhead are those of the subsidiary company United Merchants Shipping Co. Ltd., to which she had by then been transferred. In 1974, the company's last two British ships were sold and with her obsolescent machinery, *Castledore* was disposed of to breakers in Japan. *[Paul Boot]*

THOMAS A (below)
Loradore was Michalinos's first motor-ship and was completed just two years after *Castledore*. She was one of the first of their new ships to be sold however and moved to the fleet of Empros Lines Shipping Co. in 1966 as *Aliartos*. Four years later she became *Thomas A* for the new and rapidly expanding Prodromos Shipping Co., and yet a further sale between Greek principals took her in 1975 to Tsakos Shipping and Trading S.A. Her career with them as *Irene's Banner* lasted only until January 1978 when she was beached at Port Harcourt after being gutted by fire. *[George Gould/World Ship Society Ltd]*

PEGASUS (above)
Principally tanker builders, Furness Shipbuilding Co. Ltd. also constructed a few tramps for their Greek clients. Their design was characterised by an extended forecastle embracing the number 1 hold; goalpost masts and a generously-sized superstructure, as well displayed by *Pegasus* inward bound to Rotterdam in May 1971. Rethymnis and Kulukundis Ltd. initially registered her in Monrovia but she transferred to the Greek flag in 1959 which was retained after her sale in 1972 when she became *Kavo Matapas*. Subsequent names were *Yat Lung* and *Eastern Sea,* and she was broken up in Pakistan during 1983. *[George Gould/World Ship Society Ltd.]*

retained Liberian registry after her sale in 1975, finally taking the Greek colours in 1977 as *Fay C.* as which she was scrapped in 1983. *[David Salisbury]*

ATLAS (below)
Michael Xylas established his Faros Shipping Co. Ltd. in 1949 with offices in Bevis Marks, London, but had only four ships built in Britain; all by Readheads. *Atlas,* the third to be completed, joined the earlier *Anax* (8,519/1955) registered to Anax Shipping Co. S.A. of Panama; alone

ATLANTIC FURY (right)
Three almost identical ships were built for Stavros Livanos, who initially registered them under their British subsidiary company, Trent Maritime Co. Ltd. All three were later transferred to Greek or Liberian companies; *Duke of Mistra* becoming *Atlantic Fury* in 1962 as seen here in March 1974. As *Prosperity* she

amongst his other single-ship companies in having two vessels under its command. She passed to other Greek owners in 1973 as *Kapetan Xilas* and briefly went under the Honduran flag in 1979 as *Moajil 5.* In September the following year she was one of several vessels badly damaged at Umm Qasr during the Iraq–Iran war and was declared a constructive total loss and later scrapped in India under the name *Bhojani II.* *[George Gould/World Ship Society Ltd.]*

POLYXENE C (above)
Coulouthros Ltd. managed a significant fleet of mainly dry-cargo ships from their London office but had only three ships built in Britain. *Polyxene C.* was the second of the two constructed at Swan Hunter's Neptune yard. A stylish and well equipped ship she was more worthy of cargo-liner status than humble tramp and would have been well suited to charter work. As this May 1971 photograph shows she was no less well maintained. On this occasion she was employed carrying grain, much of which was still then shipped in general cargo vessels, and she is discharging at Joseph Rank's mill at Birkenhead. Two years later she was sold to Pacific International Lines (Pte) Ltd., of Singapore and as *Kota Fajar* served them until 1983 when she was demolished in India. *[Paul Boot]*

PARNASSOS (middle)
Aegean Island, the third of the British-built Coulouthros ships, came from Burntisland Shipbuilding Co. Ltd. Sailing under the Greek and later Liberian flags she was sold on to other Greek owners in 1969. As *Parnassos* she joined a small group of former British owned tramps under the management of Helikon Shipping Enterprises Ltd. whose offices too were in London. Her tramping days ended in October 1978 when she was beached at Bizerta after developing leaks during a voyage from Rotterdam to Calcutta. *[Roy Kittle]*

MARGO (bottom)
Burntisland also built four well-appointed tramps for Phocean Ship Agency Ltd. When photographed on the New Waterway in August 1976 *Margo* was still flying the Liberian flag but she moved to the Greek registry the following year. Sold in 1980 she became first *Link Love,* and later *Comet* for the delivery trip to Indian breakers in 1984. *[David Salisbury]*

238

KING THESEUS (above)
The Nomikos family had extensive shipping interests and in 1937 established a British Agency, Nomikos (London) Ltd. *King Theseus* was one of just two ships they had built in Britain, both by Blyth Dry Docks and Shipbuilding Co. Ltd. She alone was placed under the British flag, registered to Dalhousie Steam and Motorship Co. Ltd. This was to be another short term arrangement however and three years later, in 1960, *King Theseus* was transferred to the Greek flag under the ownership of Perseus Hellenic Maritime Co. Ltd. Under subsequent names of

Theotokos and *World Shelter* she lasted until 1985 when she was demolished in India. *King Theseus* is pictured leaving Rotterdam in July 1972 bound for Red Sea ports with construction equipment prominent on the fore-deck. *[George Gould/World Ship Society Ltd.]*

HELLENIC GLORY (below)
Perikles Callimanopulos, who had established his company in 1920, was unusual amongst Greek shipowners in operating regular services with conference rights both within the Mediterranean and to the USA. His ships traded under the title of Hellenic

Lines Ltd. and carried their colours, although many were actually registered to other companies. London agents were the Fenton Steamship Co. Ltd., with which our editor disclaims any connection. Just two ships were built in the United Kingdom, both by William Hamilton, and placed in the ownership of a new company Transpacific Carriers Corporation. *Hellenic Glory* and her sistership *Hellenic Torch* (7,510/56) had parallel careers, both being sold in 1982 becoming *Leader* and *Challenge,* respectively as which they were despatched to breakers. *[David Salisbury]*

LORD GLADSTONE (above)
Scotts of Greenock, the oldest family shipbuilders in Britain, constructed an interesting assortment of naval and merchant ships. Cargo liners and tankers for British companies predominated but they also won several orders from George Nicolau Ltd. *Lord Gladstone* was the last of three tramps for Norships Ocean Carriers Ltd., managed by his London based Ships Finance and Management Co. Ltd. but carrying Nicolau's prominent blue 'N' on the funnel. An enlarged version of the earlier ships, she has an unusual arrangement with four holds ahead of the superstructure. In 1969 she was transferred to the Greek flag as *N. Zografia* and sold in 1975 becoming *Constantinos T.* A succession of new owners and names followed: *Capetan Costis, Styliani, Maldive Privilege* and briefy *Dynasty Hura* as which she went to Bangaldesh breakers in 1984. *[George Gould/World Ship Society Ltd.]*

DORIEFS (left)
Like Scotts, Cammell Laird produced a wide variety of ships but just a few tramps post war, three of which were for companies managed by S. G. Embiricos. *Doriefs* was the second of the two built for Z.L. and G.L. Cambanis and she carried their distinctive blue ball on an aluminium-silver funnel band. She spent the first twenty of her 22 years with Cambanis under the Liberian flag, transferring to the Greek register in 1978. Following her sale two years later she became *Eastern Success* and was broken up at Chittagong in 1983. *[Roy Kittle]*

IRIS (above)
Doris, the earlier and smaller ship built for Cambanis, appeared in 'Record 8'. After her sale in 1973 to the Syros Shipping Company of L .M. Valmas and Son, *Iris* became quite a regular visitor to the Mersey, loading soda ash at Partington on the Manchester Ship Canal for South Africa and is seen here waiting to enter Eastham Locks in August 1976. She later became *Kastro K* and then *Stepon* as which she was broken up at Gadani Beach in 1984. *[Paul Boot]*

CANADA WITH ICE

Photos from Marc Piché

Marc Piché's photographs on an icy St. Lawrence which appeared in 'SD14: the Full Story' impressed the Ships in Focus team so much that we asked him for a further selection. We begin with a British turbine steamer in an ethereal setting of ice and steam. Cairn Line's *Cairngowan* (7,503/1951) approaches Montréal in February 1968 with ice evident well up her hull plating. She had recently been seen in Canadian waters in a different guise, on charter to Manchester Liners as *Manchester Engineer*. *Cairngowan* was sold in 1969 and broken up as *Georgilis* in Spain four years later. *[Marc Piché collection]*

The two newsprint carriers pictured on this page were managed by Runciman (London) Ltd. on behalf of a consortia of British newspaper proprietors, although later in life they passed to Canadian owners, remaining under the UK flag. *Caslon* (5,684/1949) is pictured above stuck in the ice off

Pugwash in March 1963. She was sold in 1964, becoming first *Nina G* then *Orient Transporter.* In 1970 she sustained severe damage to her steam turbines which left her fit only for use as a barge.

Below her newer running mate *Baskerville* (5,805/1954) is seen

leaving Pugwash, Nova Scotia in February 1962. Built at South Shields, the steamer remained in the fleet until 1967 when she went first to Neapolitan owners as *Irolli* and then to a Hong Kong company as *Glenealy.* She was broken up at Kaohsiung in 1974. *[Both John Low, Marc Piché collection]*

Completing a trio of newsprint carriers is *Sarah Bowater*, pictured above working hard to penetrate the ice to reach the Bowater's mill at Corner Brook, Newfoundland in March 1963, her green hull showing well against the ice. *Sarah Bowater* (6,471/1955) was the second ship built for the Bowater Steamship Co. Ltd., although the parent company had owned ships since 1925. Turbine steamers did not enjoy long lives after leaving their first owners, and only three years after her sale in 1968 this fine ship was broken up at Kaohsiung as *Grand Trader*. *[John Low, Marc Piché collection]*

Ice makes interesting patterns on the hull of *Manchester City* (8,734/1964) as she claws her way towards Montréal in February 1970 (below). One of three sister cargo liners built for Manchester Liners in the 1960s, she did not survive this line's early containerisation of its Canadian trade, and in 1971 she went to Korean owners. Under the bizarre name *One West No. 8* she was demolished at Pusan in 1985. *[Marc Piché collection]*

A travel-stained *Metallurg Anosov* (12,285/1962) appears to be straining to push through the St. Lawrence ice off Verchères in December 1980 (top). This big Kherson-built turbine steamer was a member of a large class of ice-strengthened cargo ships for work in the Soviet Arctic, the latter members of which had deck cranes rather than derricks. She was broken up in China in 1986. *[Marc Piché]*
The ice has left a mark like a massive bow wave on the hull of *Mormacpenn* (7,909/1946) downbound on the St. Lawrence River off Verchères in December 1967 (left). The Moore-McCormack C3-S-A5 type turbine steamer was sold to become *Silver Lark* in 1970 and was broken up in Taiwan during 1972. *[John Low, Marc Piché collection]*
Stefan Batory (15,044/1952) makes her last sailing of the year from the St. Lawrence on 9th December 1976 whilst still running her liner service between Montréal and Gdansk (below). The former *Maasdam* became simply *Stefan* in 1989, and lasted until demolished at Aliaga in 2000. *[Marc Piché]*

Lauritzen's polar ships were no strangers to harsh conditions but the *Saima Dan* (3,065/1962) appears marooned in a sea of ice off Varennes in the St. Lawrence near Montréal in February 1968 (above). Sold in 1975, as the Greek *Kostas K* the Dutch-built motor ship was demolished at Eleusis in 1986. *[John Low, Marc Piché collection]*

Yunn Ming (7,331/1957) shows evidence on her bow of a close encounter with an iceberg: note the crew shovelling ice off the forecastle. She was photographed arriving at Sorel in February 1976 (right). This Taiwanese motor ship had been built in Japan as *Hai Min* and was owned by Yangming Marine Transport Corporation, now a major container ship operator. As *Ming Unity* she was broken up in Taiwan in 1979. *[Marc Piché collection]*

A thin layer of ice poses no problem for *Saurel* (1,176/1929) as she runs up the St. Lawrence River near Québec City in February 1963. The veteran icebreaker and navaids tender was broken up in 1968. *[John Low, Marc Piché collection]*

Snow, ice and Newfoundland forest make a splendid backdrop for *Imperial Sarnia* (4,947/1948) near Corner Brook in February 1962 (above). The Canadian-built and owned turbine tanker is seen in the original colours of Imperial Oil Ltd. In 1987, she was acquired by Provmar Fuels of Hamilton, Ontario, who had her converted to an oil storage facility under the name of *Provmar Terminal II.* Although she will never sail again, she still provides fuel storage and transfer services in Hamilton. *[John Low, Marc Piché collection]*

The laker *J.N. McWatters* (17,591/1961) appears to be ploughing through the ice as she passes Verchères and makes her way up the St. Lawrence River towards Montréal (where she had been built) to lay up for the remainder of the winter (below). The date is 29th December 1989 and the owners Misener Shipping Ltd. *[Marc Piché]*

Norman Mcleod Rogers (4,179/1969) is making easy progress through broken ice near Québec Bridge in January 1981 (above). With a multiple role as icebreaker, buoy and supply tender, this vessel had an unusual combination of propelling machinery, consisting of diesels and gas turbines driving electric motors. In 1995 she was sold to the Chilean Navy and acquired the even longer name *Contralmirante Oscar Viel Toro*. [Marc Piché collection]

The Canadian Government icebreaker *N.B. McLean* (3,254/1930) is seen right at work on the St. Lawrence River near Trois-Rivières in March 1966. She was broken up at Kaohsiung in 1989. [John Low, Marc Piché collection]

N.B. McLean is seen again with *Indigirka* (7,661/1957) giving a helping hand in clearing ice from the Port of Montréal in March 1967. Dutch-built for the USSR, *Indigirka* was one of three icebreaking cargo ships with diesel-electric propulsion. Note her prominent crow's nest on the foremast. She was demolished in Russia in 1982. [Marc Piché collection]

KATERINA. A's HALF CENTURY

Nigel Jones and Paul Boot

There are few ships that survive much beyond 25 years. If obsolescence, structural weaknesses, mechanical problems or accidents have not already brought about its demise, then the cost and rigours of putting it through the special surveys become hurdles that can no longer be economically cleared. For any large vessel to make the half-century is therefore truly exceptional and particularly so for one that was built for general tramping. At the very end of 2006 the Greek registered *Katerina.A* sailed from Alicante on the inevitable one-way voyage to the metal merchants at Alang, fifty years and eight months since she had been named *Orpheus* by Mrs. Despina Gabriel and launched from the slipway at the Kieler Howaldtswerke A.G. shipyard at Kiel.

She was one of a series of similar-sized cargo ships built by this yard and one of two ordered on behalf of Lyras Brothers Ltd. Both were placed in the ownership of single-ship companies with *Orpheus* registered to the Orpheus Maritime Transport Corporation, Panama, although she flew the Greek flag with Piraeus as her port of registry. With a traditional 'midships layout on a hull of 509 feet overall length, a gross tonnage of 9,942 and powered by a seven-cylinder Sulzer oil engine, *Orpheus* was to all intents a ship of no particular distinction, but she had hidden strengths upon which

her future would depend. All of these ships had been built to a high specification and were classified for ice navigation with the hull having 32 millimetre-thick plating and longitudinal framing to the bottom and decks. The owners had also specified scantlings in excess of even Lloyd's requirements and her construction had been supervised by Despina Gabriel's husband, Alexander, for his brothers-in-law, Marcos and Costas Lyras.

Orpheus entered service in June 1956 and for the next 21 years she roamed around much of the globe doing what tramps do. Latterly she had carried several cargoes of cement to West Africa and in 1976 was one of over four hundred ships anchored off Apapa, Lagos waiting to discharge there. This would prove to be a foretaste of her future career.

By 1977 *Orpheus* was the oldest ship in the Lyras fleet - her sister *Phoevos* having been sold off three years previously – and she too passed to new owners: Maritime Co. Esperides S.A. Renamed *Nireus,* she was managed by the Golden Union Shipping Co. S.A. whose principals were Theodore Veniamis and Alexander Gabriel's son, George. Voyage records for the period suggest that cement was again often carried. Five years on and having now reached the usual age for retirement, it was determined that the engine and hull

Top: *Katerina. A* arriving at Alicante with her last cargo of cement on 27th November 2006.
Left: Captain Elsayed Abdelmawgoud El Soliman on the bridge of *Katerina. A.* He had been her regular master for much of her time with Horus Shipping.
Right: A view of the aft deck showing one of the reloaders installed on the former hatchways. All the reloaders were located towards the port side.
[all: Nigel Jones]

Orpheus at Apapa in January 1976 waiting to discharge her cargo of bagged cement. She was just one of the many ships anchored off the port at that time and would spend almost twelve months there.
[Malcolm Cranfield]

were still in excellent condition, with little corrosion or wastage in the steelwork, and that she would be eminently suitable for conversion into a cement handling ship.

The conversion, which would effectively double her life, was carried out at Perama during 1982 and was particularly interesting, leaving *Nireus* virtually unchanged externally with even the full set of masts and derricks retained. Each of the holds was sealed off at 'tween deck level and the weather deck hatch openings plated over. At the bottom of the holds the tank-tops were over-plated to form an inclined hopper arrangement which, in conjunction with compressed-air partial fluidisation of the cement cargo, allowed easy discharge by pipe. The key to the unloading system was a set of what are termed reloaders, supplied by the Swedish specialist cement handling company H.W.Carlsen. These were large pressure vessels with a capacity of 12 tonnes each, connected to a suction pump and compressors. They operated by alternately creating a partial vacuum in the vessel to fill a 'loading bag' in the lower section with cement sucked through a pipe from the hold and then pressuring it to evacuate the contents through a discharge line to the shore facility. There were five reloaders in total, installed on top of the plated hatch covers, with four of them operating as two tandem pairs, allowing almost continuous discharge. A typical rate of handling was around 200 tonnes per hour which, with the minimum attendance required, could be undertaken 24 hours a day, regardless of weather conditions. Apart from the reloaders, a range of auxiliary equipment (three additional auxiliary generators; three main, and two air-control compressors; one Nash vacuum pump and two Aerzener blowers) was required and this was neatly installed in the otherwise unused 'tween deck spaces together with the associated pipework and valving. Two of the derricks were retained in working order to handle the discharge pipes and for other general duties; the others just left unrigged.

Thus kitted out, *Nireus* was to spend the next three years in her new role berthed at Al Haql, a modern port just south of Aqaba in Saudi Arabia, with Heracles General Cement Co. (whose subsidiary company Eviesk S.A. had carried out the conversion) taking over the management in 1984. On completion of the contract in 1986, *Nireus* was dry-docked at Piraeus and returned to an active life taking, and self-discharging, cement cargoes to a variety of eastern Mediterranean ports. January 1987 saw her revert to a sedentary role as a storage and handling vessel, this time at Damietta at the northern end of the Gulf of Suez, where she remained until September 1991.

By this time, and now 35 years old, it might have been expected that a full retirement was due, but it was not to be. Having spent the best part of the last ten years at rest, *Nireus* was put back into active service conveying cement to a wide range of ports and during the early 1990s visited the United Kingdom on several occasions, discharging at London and at Liverpool where the cement was transferred to another storage ship to be processed and bagged. Towards the end of 1999, Blue Circle Industries acquired a controlling interest in Heracles and *Nireus* was sold to a new company, Sarah Shipping Enterprises Ltd., and placed under the Panamanian flag. The managers were Horus Shipping Co. Ltd. which had been set up the previous year by Egyptian and Spanish principals. She was to be their first ship and was named *Katerina. A* after the mother of the Egyptian co-owner and director Mr.Azam. Trading patterns were much as before but in 2003 Horus obtained an annually renewable charter from the Levante Cement Co. for conveying cement from the Black Sea port of Novorossiysk to Alicante. For the next four years she settled into a routine cycle, taking around 25 days for the return voyage, including a call at Piraeus for bunkers, stores and provisions, that finally came to an end on 3rd December 2006 when she sailed from the Spanish port after discharging her last cargo. With the expiry of the charter and with a special survey looming in January 2007, the company decided that ship could no longer be viably traded. After calling briefly at Piraeus, *Katerina. A* was summarily dispatched to the breakers where she arrived just before Christmas and was beached early on the morning of 31st December. As the photograph of her arriving at Alicante shows, she was well maintained to the end and although obviously showing her age in places, she may well have survived a few more years if circumstances had been different.

Despite her being one of the last of her kind it is surprising that *Katerina. A* has attracted so little attention from shipping enthusiasts. Her departure raises the inevitable question: was she the last of the truly traditional cargo ships to trade in European waters?

Sources and acknowledgements
Kings of the Oceans 1948-56. George Foustanos.
Argo Publishing and Advertising Ltd., Piraeus 2000
Die Geschichte und Schicksale deutsche Serienfrachter,
Verlag Gert Uwe Detlefsen, Bad Segeberg 1998
For giving their considerable help in preparation of this article, the authors are particularly grateful to:
Captain Costas G. Kangelaris, Marine Superintendant, Horus Shipping Co.
Captain Elsayed Abdelmawgoud El Soliman, master.
Mr . George Gabriel, director Golden Union Co. S.A.
Mr. Guillermo Alberola, Roumeu & Cia., ship's agent at Alicante
Mr. Johan Riedenlow, H.W Carlsen, Malmo.

J. WHARTON (SHIPPING) LTD.

Part 2

Ken Garrett

Challenge

The establishment of a private port at Gunness constituted a considerable challenge in itself but to operate the port in an efficient manner inevitably drew the company into conflict with a number of organisations. Although close to the motorway network with excellent communications to the Midlands and other industrial centres, the company has always benefited from its relatively remote situation. The position of the head office, moved to Gunness in March 1966, and the wharves some distance from the nearest public road still presented a practical as well as psychological barrier to unwanted visitors.

This position served the company well during the dockers' strike in the early 1970s when, regardless of the wishes of the Gunness men, the wharf attracted the attention of flying pickets of registered dockers from elsewhere. Despite many angry scenes the workers at the wharf were resistant to outside interference and could see the advantages of efficiency and flexible working arrangements. This attitude was in complete contrast to their opposite numbers at the nearby scheme port of Hull where it took virtual closure and the demise of the National Dock Labour Scheme to return the port to commercial reality.

The access road proved its worth again during the miners' strike in the mid-1980s when the wharf continued to handle imports of coal from the continent brought in by foreign and non-federated British ships throughout the strike. Inevitably the wharf became the target for a number of militant groups but its isolated position and the resolution of the management and staff, with their excellent industrial relations, ensured that the wharf kept operating without interruption. It is indeed ironic that one of the busiest periods in the history of the wharf should be concerned with the import rather than the export of coal on which the company was founded.

The ships too had their problems. During the 1970s, when good British seafarers were in short supply, the company adopted a practical solution and employed some Spanish officers and seamen, particularly on the Trent Lighterage ships. Predictably this upset the British Shipping Federation and the seafarers' unions but despite some threatening noises nothing much had happened before the ships were sold.

Shipowning also brought the company into occasional conflict with the local pilots. The company held that their masters, mostly local men who made regular voyages into the Trent, were more experienced than the licensed pilots and thus quite capable of piloting their own ships. This was probably true but the pilots were able to invoke the terms of the 1913 Pilotage Act that overlooked such practical considerations. On several occasions an unfortunate master was hauled before the local magistrates and fined for not availing himself of the services of a licensed pilot. The re-organisation of the pilotage service and new regulations has changed the situation and

although the company no longer owns any ships, the ships' agency side of the business has been active in assisting masters of regular traders to obtain the all important Pilotage Exemption Certificates.

Jersey Royals

The trade with the Channel Islands stemmed from Jack Wharton's experience as a potato trader and commenced in the early 1950s. The trade began when the *Stevonia*, *Gladonia* and *Jackonia* were chartered for several consecutive years by Channel Transporters (Portsmouth) Ltd. for the Jersey Royal potato season from May to June. They returned again in August for the outdoor tomato season and finishing in October. The cargoes were loaded at Albert Pier in St. Helier harbour and discharged at the Camber Quay in Portsmouth. The ships generally made three round trips a week. When two ships were operating, they would alternate with one sailing from Jersey on Monday, Wednesday and Friday and the running mate sailing on Tuesday, Thursday and Saturday.

A profile view of the *Gladonia (1)*. [J. and M. Clarkson collection]

In later years, during the full season, four ships would operate the service with one large and one smaller ship each day, e.g. *Trentonia* (2) with *Gladonia* (2) and *Brendonia* (3) with *Ecctonia*. The ships would endeavour to sail together and there were often wagers on which would be the first to arrive. The important thing was to get the produce to Portsmouth for the market and although risks were taken to keep to the schedule there were few mishaps.

J.W. Huelin Ltd. had started to ship produce from Jersey to Portsmouth in 1953 and had chartered two Dutch coasters, *Bill-S* (499/1947) and *Maymere* (499/1946). The following year, 1954, the long association between Huelins and Whartons began when the *Stevonia* came on charter in June for the potato season to be joined in September by *Gladonia* for the outdoor tomatoes. In most cases the ships returned empty and in ballast to Jersey but occasionally they had a return cargo of straw. By 1957, although not large enough on her own for Huelin's increasing share of the potato trade, the *Stevonia* stayed on and carried tomatoes until the start of the new cauliflower trade in November. This season continued until March 1958 and return cargoes of building materials became a regular feature. By this time the loading berth had changed to the New North Pier and later still to the Victoria Pier.

The potato, tomato, broccoli and cauliflower seasons, being dependent upon the weather, did not always run into each other and thus there were often gaps in the charters. The ship to resume the charter was therefore the one in the best position with the result that most of the company's ships were involved at one time or another.

In the autumn of 1958 the following announcement was made in the Jersey local press: 'Commencing mid November 1958, J.W. Huelin Ltd. will resume their broccoli service with sailings on Tuesdays and Fridays. Captain Mitchell who has made 150 sailings in *Stevonia* under our produce charter will now command the British *Trentonia*. Last season we carried two thirds of all the broccoli and this year we will do even better.'

Gladonia started a run to Shoreham during the 1960 potato season, this was repeated the following year but with disappointing results and was discontinued. Other exceptional cargoes were carried from time to time; for example, *Trentonia* following a cargo of cement from London in February 1963 loaded a cargo of specially hewn granite blocks for the doorway of Jack Wharton's new house 'Trentlands' then being built at Burton-upon-Stather. The same ship carried 40 pigs from Jersey to St. Malo in November 1963 returning with cider apples in bulk.

New buildings at Goole

While the produce trade was running its course, the need was felt to replace some of the older and mainly second-hand ships with some new buildings. To favour local industry, the orders were placed with the shipyard at Goole with the requirement that local Appleby Frodingham steel should be used in the construction. Lister Blackstone engines and Macgregor steel hatch covers were specified which, with other items, ensured that there was a very high percentage of British content in the ships.

Four ships were ordered, two each for J. Wharton Shipping and Trent Lighterage. They were allocated the yard numbers 539, 540, 547 and 552. The first pair, *Gladonia* (2) and *Ecctonia*, came into service in 1963 and had a deadweight of 906 tons. To ease the stowage of produce pallets the holds were given flush tank tops and small bilge wells instead of the more traditional inclined limbers covering a continuous bilge along each side of the ship.

Yard number 539, the first ship to be built for Trent Lighterage, was launched by Mrs J. Eccles. There had been considerable debate to find a suitable name for the ship to combine the major shareholders' names whilst retaining the established Wharton style. A strong contender had been *Ecclestonia* but happily this was abbreviated to the punchy and less cumbersome *Ecctonia*.

The second pair, *Trentonia* (2) and *Brendonia* (3), were somewhat smaller with a deadweight of 837 tons. This enabled owner and charterer to ring the changes of ships on the produce run to suit the volume of cargo. When the trade was in full swing the ships would operate in two pairs, one large and one small to give flexibility, and when things started to slow down it was easy to adjust the tonnage allocated to the trade. When the two ships were sold in 1984 there was a usual clause in the sale agreements that the new owner would change the ship's name. Some minor irritation was caused when this was carried out in an economical manner and the two became *Trenton* and *Brendonian* thus maintaining the word if not the spirit of the agreement. The irritation increased when a request to the Registrar General to name a later ship *Brendonia* was refused on the grounds that it was too similar to *Brendonian*.

Gladonia (2), the first of the four Goole-built ships. [J. K. Byass/Roy Fenton collection]

Left: The launch of the *Ecctonia* at Goole. *[Company archives]*

Below: *Trentonia* (2) at Jersey. *[Dave Hocquard]*

Above: Huelin funnel motif as seen on the *Trentonia* (2). *[Dave Hocquard]*

The produce trade - peak and decline

By 1964 *Trentonia* was chartered all the year round and carried the Huelin funnel mark. Motor vehicles and general cargo were added to the return cargoes of building materials, and sometimes an intermediate call was made at Guernsey to discharge part of the cargo. In October that year, while lying at St.Helier, her name was changed to *Trentonia II* to release her name for the new ship being built at Goole.

The new *Trentonia* (2) went straight into the Huelin produce trade and carried the charterer's funnel mark when she came into service in November 1964. A milestone was reached in January 1968 when Captain Arthur Mitchell made his 1,000th produce voyage. He had commanded three ships on the trade, *Stevonia*, *Trentonia* (1) and *Trentonia* (2). There were great celebrations to mark the event and the ship had to stand off St. Helier for a while until all the welcoming party were fully assembled.

Eventually the increasing volume of the produce trade, by this time palletised, coupled with a considerable growth in the return cargoes and the natural requirement for ever faster turnrounds prompted the charterer, now known as Huelin (Jersey) Ltd., to take some 'tween deckers on charter in late 1969. The less flexible *Trentonia* and her single-deck sisters carried on for a while but the last produce voyage was made in July 1971. Originally the trade was quite a moneyspinner but unfortunately the freight rates had not gone up in step with costs. Although Jack Wharton, when on holiday on the island, used to delight in driving to La Corbiere on a summer evening to watch his ships sail past, sentiment was no longer sufficient reason to maintain a service that had so dominated the company's operations for 21 years.

Tragedy

The sinking of the *Burtonia* in 1972 with the loss of four lives came as a severe blow to the company and there were widespread repercussions as the recommendations of the inevitable Court of Enquiry were implemented.

The ship loaded a cargo of 558 tons of lead concentrate, consigned to Ghent, at Railway Wharf, Keadby where work had commenced on 27th November. The cargo was brought to the wharf in lorries from the Cavendish Mill of Laporte Industries Ltd. at Eyam in Derbyshire where the concentrate was produced by the froth flotation process from locally mined fluorspar ore. Naturally some moisture would be retained and such cargoes were known to be dangerous in the sense that if too wet they could liquefy under the combined influence of ship movement and engine vibration. In this condition the cargo could slide to one side of the hold causing a dangerous list from which the ship would be unlikely to recover. The contemporary Bulk Cargoes Code of the Intergovernmental Maritime Consultative Organisation (IMCO) required that the material should be tested to determine the moisture content necessary to cause it to shear under controlled vibration. The actual moisture content of the cargo to be shipped must not exceed 90% of that figure.

Loading took the pattern followed on 17 previous occasions whereby the lorries dumped the cargo on to the concrete quay from where it was loaded into the ship by mobile grabs. The grabs would ensure that the cargo was trimmed more or less level into the wings and ends of the holds. Cargo operations continued into 28th November with the final two lorries arriving inexplicably late to complete the loading in the evening. It was later stated that these two lorry loads appeared to be wetter than the rest of the cargo but nothing was reported at the time.

The hatches were covered by their wooden boards and tarpaulins, properly battened down for sea, and the ship sailed on the tide at 13.00 on the 29th. The pilot recalled that the ship was upright and everything appeared normal as she sailed down the river. The passage down the North Sea was accompanied by worsening but not particularly worrying weather conditions. Just after 20.00 when the ship was about ten miles north east of the Outer Gabbard light vessel she took some heavy seas and the

The *John M* which stood by the stricken *Burtonia*, picking up three of the crew when she sank. *[J. and M. Clarkson]*

mate, Walter Pheasant, noticed that the ship's behaviour had changed and she now had a ten degree list to starboard and was not rolling back past the upright position. The ship's relief master, Captain James Ash, came to the bridge and switching on the floodlights ascertained that the tarpaulins appeared to be intact and then altered course to the west into the south westerly gale. The situation appeared serious enough at this stage for the crew to be mustered, instructed to check that the ship was secure and to don their lifejackets.

Shortly afterwards, at 20.42, Captain Ash decided that things had deteriorated to the extent that he sent out a Mayday call. This was picked up by North Foreland Radio whose operators relayed the message. Both Harwich and Aldeburgh lifeboats were put on stand-by and the vessels *John M* (1,308/1963) and *Smithbank* (327/1970) indicated that they had picked up the call and were proceeding towards the *Burtonia*. Of the two, the *John M* was in the best position and she altered course to make a rendezvous in the vicinity of the Outer Gabbard light vessel.

At 21.48 Captain Ash made a call to the company secretary, Stan Smith, and reported his situation. He was advised to maintain contact with the *John M* as this ship seemed to offer the best hope of assistance. Shortly after this the Aldeburgh lifeboat launched and also proceeded towards the Outer Gabbard rendezvous. About this time a fateful decision was taken when the *Burtonia*, probably realising that in the prevailing conditions there was little future in pursuing her westerly course, altered course to the northward to seek the shelter of the East Anglian coast and make for Lowestoft. This action was apparently not reported by the *Burtonia* or the *John M*, by this time in visual contact. This had a crucial affect on subsequent events. Curiously this was followed at 22.39 by North Foreland Radio - apparently after consultation with Captain Ash - announcing that the status had been reduced from a Mayday to a Pan or Urgency situation.

In reality this was far from the truth: the *Burtonia*'s position and course was only known to those on board and to the shadowing *John M*, while the Aldeburgh lifeboat was battling through the weather in the wrong direction. Meanwhile the ship's situation and the weather were worsening. It was not until 01.00 on the 30th that the lifeboat coxswain, after failing to find the casualty near the light vessel, took matters into his own hands and fired a flare. This was seen by the *John M* who reported the bearing directly to the lifeboat that was then able to proceed in the right direction.

By 02.40 the situation was hopeless and Captain Ash gave the order to abandon ship which the mate reported over the radio telephone. Shortly afterwards the ship laid over on her beam ends and the *John M*, close astern, picked up the three Spanish seamen. The ship remained afloat until 03.37 when it sank about seven miles east of Benacre Ness. The mate had remained aboard until the end, when he was washed off the sinking vessel. Supported by a life buoy and an upturned life raft, he was rescued by the Aldeburgh Lifeboat which had at last reached the scene. Captain Ash had apparently died in the wheelhouse - possibly having suffered a heart attack during the confusion - and went down with his ship.

Other ships including the *Duncansby Head* (4,440/1969), *Troup Head* (1,585/1971), the tug *Wrestler* (704/1972) and HMS *Bildeston* searched the area for survivors. They were assisted later by helicopters and Hercules aircraft from the U.S. airbase at Woodbridge but were unable to find either of the two engineers or the cook.

The ensuing Court of Enquiry, lasting 43 days, found that the loss was caused by the cargo of lead concentrates shifting. Because the ship remained relatively lively almost to the end, a leak was ruled out and the shift was assumed to have been caused by the effect of a high initial moisture content.

Few of the parties involved in the tragedy escaped the criticism of the court, not least the shore-based communications and search and rescue centres and their procedures. In the event they had been found wanting because a ship was lost with loss of life only seven miles offshore and seven hours after the first report. As a result, these procedures were revised and improved; cargo testing, certification and the supply of necessary information to ships' masters and shippers was also considerably improved.

Grove Wharf

The development of the Grove Farm site proceeded steadily with the wharves, handling and storage areas being gradually extended. The head office was moved to Grove Wharf from Keadby in March 1966. Developed literally from a green field site in 1958, Grove Wharf was handling half a million tonnes of cargo annually by 1970. A large proportion of the tonnage was grain for export. Expansion took place almost immediately, and in 1971 J. Mowlem (Yorkshire) Ltd. was contracted to build a new jetty at a price of £124,000. The works were completed in five months and the new jetty was opened in November 1971 when the *Trentonia* (2) arrived to discharge silver sand from Antwerp and then loaded peat for Guernsey.

The million tonne barrier was passed in 1980 and by 1984 the annual tonnage had passed the two million mark. By this time the wharf was handling a wide variety of cargoes with specialist facilities for grain, fertilisers, animal feeds, minerals, coal and forest products including timber, pulp, paper and hardboard. On one notable occasion, British timber was loaded for export to Scandinavia.

By the time of the company centenary in 1990, an investment of more than £20 million had provided nine riverside berths at Gunness with a potential annual capacity of 3.5 million tonnes. Warehouses and surfaced storage were provided and later a specialised forest products warehouse for the Swedish SCA company. There was considerable investment in plant and equipment commensurate with getting the full advantage from the wharves. A small laboratory was built to enable shippers to sample and test the cargo. Release of materials to the receivers is computer controlled and at any moment the current situation can be reported, with lists of vehicles loaded, those waiting, cargo despatched and that still in store. The busy wharf amply demonstrates the foresight and acumen of Jack Wharton who had the wisdom to see the opportunity so many years ago.

Hardly had the celebrations to mark the new millennium become a memory when the wharf was further extended. First the purchase of the adjacent Neap House Wharf increased the number of berths to 11, and this was followed by purchase of another farm on the other side of the original site to extend the port estate almost to the village of Gunness itself.

Although the river and the tides still determine the size of ships that can use the wharf, they have gradually grown bigger since the little *Saint Enoch* crept up to Keadby in 1925. Nowadays, ships with a deadweight of over 5,000 tonnes can discharge at Gunness where the maximum draft is now 5.5 metres on springs and 4.5 metres on neap tides. While there are no restrictions on beam or air draft, the overall length is limited to 100 metres because of the need to swing in the river.

With the development of Grove Wharf, warehousing and stevedoring were added to the company's original activities of shipowning, broking and chartering. In 1961 the company started to develop a road transport operation and a fleet of articulated vehicles with bulk or flat trailers began to carry the Wharton house flag along the nation's motorways. All this activity necessitated the incorporation of several subsidiary companies: J. Wharton (Stevedoring) Ltd., J. Wharton (Transport) Ltd., J. Wharton (Warehousing) Ltd. and J. Wharton (Farmers) Ltd. all being consolidated under the parent J. Wharton (Shipping) Ltd.

Unfortunately Jack Wharton did not live to see the fruition of his plans for he died in a Jersey hospital in August 1969 leaving his son to carry on. Steven Wharton had come into the business in 1961 when he was eighteen and for some time had been handling the daily affairs due to his father's failing health. He became the managing director and was supported on the board by his mother, Mrs Gladys Wharton, his sisters Mrs Brenda Blundell and Mrs

Elizabeth Greetham and also by members of the Everard family.

Steven maintained his father's interest in farming and football and became a director of Scunthorpe United Football Club and is now its Chairman. He is a keen horseman but his early sporting interest was hockey. He played several games for the East of England and over 100 games for his native Lincolnshire where, in hockey terms, Yorkshire ends on the north shore of the Humber and Lincolnshire starts on the south shore. Humberside, North or South, never existed. Steven married Fiona Windle at St. Mary's Church, Sprotborough in October 1978 and they have two children, a daughter Angela and a son, William.

Bareboat charter

The *Jack Wharton*, by far the largest vessel ever owned by the company, was built by Richards (Shipbuilders) Ltd. of Lowestoft in 1977 to plans developed for the associated F.T. Everard and Co. Ltd. by the Swan Hunter Small Ship Division. Each aspect of the building was thoroughly discussed and none more so than the navigating bridge. The builders had proposed a fairly traditional arrangement, mainly with a view to ease of construction, whereas something better was wanted by the owners. After some argument, an advanced design was achieved that soon appeared in the builder's brochure as the 'Swan Hunter standard small ship bridge design'.

The ship had a gross tonnage of 1,597 and, by exploiting many of the loopholes in the 1967 British Tonnage Rules, a total deadweight of 4,161 was achieved. This was later increased to 4,489 tons when the British government was persuaded to accept a further loophole. This had long been employed by German owners and builders and involved extending the notional 'tween deck into the engine room and raising the forecastle deck. It is interesting to note that under the 1969 International Tonnage Convention, which eschews all such subterfuges and produces a reasonably accurate assessment of the enclosed space, the ship's new gross tonnage became 2,488.

The ship was launched by Mrs Gladys Wharton on 18th August 1977 and entered service in November. Immediately on acceptance from the builders the ship was placed on bareboat charter to F.T. Everard and Sons Ltd. and always appeared in their livery. Everard's technical staff supervised the building and the known association of the two companies encouraged various wags in the yard to chalk their

Family group at the launch of the *Jack Wharton* in August 1977. Back row: Mrs.Brenda Blundell (nee Wharton), Virginia Blundell, John Blundell, Steven Wharton, Mrs.Elizabeth Greetham (nee Wharton) and John Greetham. Front row: Robert Greetham, Victor Greetham, Mrs.Gladys Wharton, Caroline Blundell and Rebecca Greetham. *[Company archives]*

suggestions for the ship's name using imaginative combinations, some not so subtle, of the owner's and charterer's naming styles.

As built the ship turned out to be very wet on deck in even a moderate sea and had a propensity to trim by the head when loaded with an homogeneous cargo. This always made the carriage of grain cargoes a difficult affair. With light grain, the ship would be full and trim by the head, becoming awkward to handle at sea although it was sometimes possible to alleviate the situation by the use of ballast water. With heavy grain it would be possible to leave an ullage in the forward hold to achieve a good trim but the disadvantage to this was the necessity to secure the surface with several tiers of grain in bags, a very expensive process.

Jack Wharton. [Charles Hill]

The original design had incorporated a modest bulbous bow but this was deleted from the final version. By giving more buoyancy forward it might have improved the trim and made the ship easier to work. With a better water flow, a bulb would probably have resulted in a lower fuel consumption and would have reduced the wash that was most noticeable when navigating in rivers and other confined waters.

The *Jack Wharton* and her three Everard sisters initially ran on marine diesel distillate or gas oil but by the late 1970s these light fuel oils had become increasingly expensive. The effect of the high prices was very marked with these ships by comparison with purely coastal vessels because of their long sea passages and relatively short stays in port. In an attempt to retrieve the situation, the ship was converted in 1980 to burn the cheaper but heavier IFO 30 fuel oil. However, by this time the price differential was narrowing and it was found that the quality and availability of the heavier fuel was variable to say the least. Experience soon showed that due to the extra maintenance costs for the Alpha engine the anticipated savings did not fully materialise and it was not long before the *Jack Wharton* reverted to the original fuel.

It is always tempting to imbue a ship with various human qualities and none more so than luck. Without doubt some ships appear to have charmed lives and happily go their way without any major problems. It could not be said that the *Jack Wharton* was one of these fortunate craft; indeed, quite the reverse seemed to be the case. A main engine seizure in the Mediterranean forced a tow to Shoreham to discharge a cargo of pumice loaded at Lipari and thence to Rotterdam for a new engine. On another occasion, whilst raising the anchor in bad weather, the mate was injured and had to be airlifted to hospital. One of the most dramatic incidents involved the master and third engineer who went missing in the ship's BOTI boat when returning from a trip ashore at Lipari. They finally managed to beach the boat on the neighbouring island of Sicily the following evening.

A chief engineer, sent out to join the ship at Algiers, was detained by the authorities and not released until the ship had sailed. Unable to communicate with the company, he acted on his own initiative and managed to get on a flight to Paris. There was considerable relief when he reported his safe arrival.

Dock strikes and other delays dogged the ship and affected her commercial performance. It seemed at the time that through no fault of her own the ship was bound to get caught up in other people's disputes. A prime example occurred at Tilbury when a dockers' strike was called after she had loaded only a few tons of wheat at the grain terminal and she was forced to stay there idle and strikebound for ten days. Elsewhere, anchored off Algiers as an 'arrived ship' and awaiting a berth, she was clocking up demurrage at a higher rate than she could possibly have otherwise earned, when the agent, apparently acting on his own, told the ship to proceed to Ghazouet to discharge. Unfortunately the master accepted the orders without consulting the company and that ruined the demurrage claim so that all the time had been wasted. Throughout her life with the company the ship had more than her fair share of mechanical problems. On one voyage from mid-December to mid-January she sailed from Mobile bound for Monrovia. In addition to several days spent repairing in Miami and Trinidad, she had many stops at sea along the way which when added together came to a total of 22 days.

But despite all this, with her sister vessels the *Jack Wharton* extended the charterer's activities that had previously not gone much further than Archangel in the north and the Mediterranean in the south. The company secretary suggested to the charterers that the ship should load a cargo for Gunness but a few years were still to elapse before it was considered safe for such a large ship to visit the port. She made several voyages to the eastern seaboard of Canada and the USA, also to the Azores, Caribbean and Guyana, West Africa and one voyage through the Suez canal to Yenbo. Considered for trading into the Great Lakes, it had to be conceded that the design was too compact to permit the fitting of the winches and other gear required for transit of the Seaway.

Once hostilities had ceased in the Falklands, the ship was fitted with a load-bearing 'tween deck and joined her sisters in taking military stores and equipment to Ascension and Port Stanley. Having just one 20-ton crane in the centre and a 5-ton crane at the end of each hold, her usefulness was limited but for a few years she was sorely needed.

Eventually, when the 'demerger' took place in 1986, the *Jack Wharton* together with the other vessels in the J. Wharton (Shipping) Ltd. fleet were transferred to Everards. Permission was granted by the Registrar of Shipping to change the name to *Similarity* but she was sold to Charles Willie (Shipping) Ltd. of Cardiff before the renaming was carried out. Sold again to Greek and other owners, one is bound to wonder whether the ship's luck changed.

Top: *Gladonia (2) [Jean M. Otten/Roy Fenton collection]*
Bottom: *Brendonia (3)* 3rd September 1966. *[John G. Callis/Roy Fenton collection]*

Fleet list part 2

The list follows the usual Ships in Focus format, with the addition of port number and any relevant Commonwealth or foreign official numbers.

8. GLADONIA (2) 1963-1985
3/1963 Goole.
O.N. 300230 657.78g 346.95n 906d
56.80 x 9.07 x 3.70 metres.
8-cyl 4SCSA oil engine made by Lister Blackstone Marine Ltd., Dursley. 222 x 292 mm; 492 kW, 10 knots.
17.9.1963: Completed by Goole Shipbuilding and Repairing Co. Ltd., Goole (Yard No. 540) for J. Wharton (Shipping) Ltd., Gunness as GLADONIA.
18.3.1985: Sold to Liberty Exports Ltd.

(Jenkins Garages (Southerndown) Ltd., managers), Bridgend, renamed INTEGRITY and provisionally registered in Honduras.
19.1.1987: Sold to Runwave Shipping Ltd. (Ian Roberts, manager), Avonmouth and renamed GLADONIA.
4.2.1987: Re-registered in Gibraltar 17/1987. O.N. 300230.
26.1.1990: Re-registered in St.Vincent and the Grenadines. O.N. 2814.
19.7.1994: Tonnages, ITC'69, became 630g, 328n, 906d.
9.1994: Sold to Rose Navigation Ltd., Kingstown, St. Vincent and the Grenadines (Mustafa Badr, Barcelona, Spain, manager).
1997: Renamed SAMARET JAMA and re-registered in Belize.
31.12.1999: Foundered in heavy weather at Puerto Cabello, Venezuela.

9. BRENDONIA (3) 1966-1984
1/1966 Goole.
O.N. 306452 604.19g 301.77n 837d
54.03 x 9.10 x 3.61 metres.
8-cyl 4SCSA oil engine made by Lister Blackstone Marine Ltd., Dursley; 222 x 292 mm; 492 kW, 10.5 knots.
23.5.1966: Completed by Goole Shipbuilding and Repairing Co. Ltd., Goole (Yard No. 552) for J. Wharton (Shipping) Ltd., Gunness as BRENDONIA.
8.5.1984: Sold to Whiting (Shipping) Ltd., Great Yarmouth.
21.10.1984: Renamed BRENDONIAN.
18.7.1994: Tonnages, ITC'69, became 587g, 296n, 837d.
3.2000: Sold to Inter Oceanic Maritime Shipping Inc., Barranquilla, Columbia,

renamed SHASKIA LEE and registered in Panama.
3.2004: Renamed SEA SONG.
3.2005: Sold to Sea Cargo Interoceanic S.A., Barranquilla, Columbia and renamed OCEAN SONG.
8.2006: Still in service.

10. JACK WHARTON 1977-1986
3/1977 Goole.
O.N. 364572 1,597.02g 1056.64n 4,161d
89.72 x 14.28 x 6.04 metres.
18-cyl 4SCSA 'V' oil engine made by Alpha-Diesel A/S, Frederikshavn, Denmark; 225 x 300 mm; 2,081 kW, 13 knots.
1.11.1977: Completed by Richards (Shipbuilders) Ltd., Lowestoft (Yard No. 532) for J. Wharton (Shipping) Ltd., Gunness as JACK WHARTON and bareboat chartered to F.T. Everard and Sons Ltd., Greenhithe.
30.6.1986: Owner became F.T. Everard Shipping Ltd., Greenhithe.

Brendonia in Albert Dock, Hull on 11th March 2000 as she was being renamed *Shaskia Lee.* [George Robinson]

Middle: *Jack Wharton* in the English Channel in Everard colours. [FotoFlite, 286136]
Bottom left: *Jack Wharton.* [W. J. Harvey] Bottom right: As the *Celtic Ambassador.* [FotoFlite, 74887]

257

Above: *Ecctonia* in the Ouse below Goole. *[Charles Hill]* Below left: In drydock at Goole on 22nd July 1984. Below right: Sailing from the Manchester Ship Canal at Eastham on 16th July 1987 as the *Vasa Sound*. *[Both: Mike Ridgard]*

16.2.1987: Sold to Charles M. Willie (Shipping) Ltd., Cardiff and renamed CELTIC AMBASSADOR. Registered 2/1987 in Cardiff.
26.4.1990: Sold to Oceanlaser Shipping Ltd., Limassol, Cyprus (Stavros Roussos Management and Chartering S.A., Piraeus, Greece, managers) and renamed SMARO. O.N. 709053.
1993: Sold to Crestwave Shipping S.A., Panama (Pan Nautic S.A., Lugano, Switzerland, managers), renamed RICCAM and registered in Panama. Tonnages, ITC'69, became 2,488g, 1,627n, 4,161d.
1996: Sold to Stanford Shipping S.A., Panama (Pan Nautic S.A., Lugano, Switzerland, managers), renamed AMBASSADOR 1 and registered in Panama.
1998: Renamed CLAMBA and registered in Madeira (Portugal).
2001: Sold to M.S. Enterprises International Ltd., Singapore (Erico Shipping Co. Ltd. Nakhodka, Russia,

manager), renamed CAPTAIN RAFFLES and registered in Pnom-Penh, Cambodia.
12.2004: Renamed FERDINAND.
8.2006: Still in service.

Managed ships

T3. ECCTONIA 1963-1986
2/1963 Goole
O.N. 300229 657.78g 347.95n 906d
56.80 x 9.07 x 3.70 metres.
8-cyl 4SCSA oil engine made by Lister Blackstone Marine Ltd., Dursley, 222 x 292 mm; 492 kW, 10 knots.
9.7.1963: Completed by Goole Shipbuilding and Repairing Co. Ltd., Goole (Yard No. 539) for Trent Lighterage Ltd. (J. Wharton (Shipping) Ltd., managers), Gunness as ECCTONIA.
4.11.1986: Sold to Dennison Shipping Ltd., Kirkwall, Orkney.
10.2.1987: Renamed VASA SOUND and registered 2/1987 in Kirkwall.
22.11.1990: Struck rocks at Bogha Nuadh

in the Firth of Lorne while on passage from Loch Aline to Ardrossan with a cargo of sand. Temporary repairs carried out at Ipswich.
12.1990: Declared a constructive total loss and proceeded to Goole where she arrived on 30.12.1990.
18.3.1991: Sold to Runwave Shipping Ltd. (Ian Roberts, manager), Avonmouth.
3.1991: Sold to F.C. Larkham and G.H. Cook, Westbury-on-Severn and laid up at Sharpness.
1993: Renamed SOUND and registered in Kingstown, St. Vincent and the Grenadines.
1994: Sold to V. Whale Ltd. (Ricky Lee Paul, manager), Hong Kong and renamed SEA LION 5.
1995: Transferred to Sealion Ltd. (Ricky Lee Paul, manager), Hong Kong, registered in San Lorenzo, Honduras and converted into a live fish carrier.
2002: Deleted from Lloyd's Register as continued existence in doubt.

T4. TRENTONIA (2) 1964-1984
1/1964 Goole.
O.N. 300232 604.19g 301.51n 837d
54.03 x 9.10 x 5.61 metres.
8-cyl 4SCSA oil engine made by Lister
Blackstone Marine Ltd., Dursley, 222 x
292 mm; 492 kW, 10.5 knots.
28.11.1964: Completed by Goole
Shipbuilding and Repairing Co. Ltd.,
Goole (Yard No. 547) for Trent Lighterage

Ltd. (J. Wharton (Shipping) Ltd.,
managers), Gunness as TRENTONIA.
21.4.1984: Sold to Alan Peter Whiting and
Susan Mary Whiting, Strood and renamed
TRENTON.
20.2.1986: Registered 11/1986 in
Guernsey.
13.9.1988: Sole owner became Alan Peter
Whiting, Maidstone. Registered 34/1988
in Hull.

2.7.1991: Sold to Rashid bin Rashid,
Bahrain.
1992: Owner became Rashid
Establishment, Bahrain.
1993: Sold to Jaleel, Sharjah, United Arab
Emirates. Registered in Bahrain.
8.2006: Still in service.

To be concluded.

Trentonia (2) [J. K. Byass/Roy Fenton collection]

RECORD REVIEWS

THE TYSER LEGACY: A HISTORY OF PORT LINE by Ian Farquhar
376-page hardback published by the New Zealand Ships and Marine Society at £30.
Distributed in Europe by Ships in Focus.

It has been a long time coming but it has arrived at last: the history of Port Line and its antecedents. This will become the standard work on the company that seemed to epitomise the very best that was British cargo liner shipping. Up until its sublimation into the container revolution, Port Line engendered a level of affection amongst its staff ashore and afloat, its cargo shipping customers and the yards that built the ships that was almost without equal.

'The Tyser Legacy' is no elaborated fleet list of some notable ships. It is the punch-packed saga of men and means, engineers and seamen, shipbuilders and shippers. The common thread was imaginative constructive ambition. Here are described freight wars and conference rights. There are stories of pooling agreements and living with governments' parastatals in over-governed Australia and New Zealand that produced 'boards' that tried to control exports that were as large as dairy produce and as small as canned fruit. Graphically described is how the Vesteys, with their Blue Star Line afloat and their meat works ashore, bullied their way into almost every route and trade that they targeted: even the might of P&O Group with their local presence in the form of Federal, New Zealand Shipping, Avenue, British India and P&O itself could not block the Vesteys' relentlessness. No history of a shipping enterprise serving Australasia would be complete without mention of the woes of the waterfront and the dominant expansive stupidities of the Wharfies - not that the London dockers were much better. How did shipowners stay sane when in 1951, beset by industrial disputes in New Zealand, *Port Vindex (*1949) was on the New Zealand coast for 157 days and *Port Auckland* (1949) for 135 days: the average was 60 days.

Ian Farquhar starts his narrative with how the Tyser family first came to build a fleet of sailing ships and then gained contracts for the carriage of frozen meat from New Zealand in chartered steamers. The enterprise of the Tysers of London, the Roydens of Liverpool, the Corrys of Belfast and the Milburns of Newcastle-upon-Tyne, all being of like minds, drew together for commercial and operational reasons to benefit the expansion of trade as Australia and New Zealand emerged from being crown colonies into self-governing dominions and onwards as part of the British Commonwealth. By 1905 a group of lines led by Tysers and also using vessels from the fleets of Milburn, Royden, Corry and even Houston Line, were able to offer a weekly sailing in the seven-month-long Australian wool season from the range of loading ports to Britain and Europe. Just ahead of the outbreak of the First World War the four partners formed the Commonwealth and Dominion Line and consolidated their interests in one company. Only two years later Thomas Royden, as a director of Cunard, brokered a deal valued at £5,000,000 in which Cunard on secret terms acquired all the Commonwealth and Dominion shares: the value of the company had doubled in just two years. Cunard wanted to become less dependent on trans-Atlantic trades.

With the might of Cunard behind them, the well-tried and tested unchanged Port Line management moved into diesel-engined ships with *Port Dunedin* in 1925 after which they never built another steam-powered ship. Here was new technology capable of powering a 7,463gt ship at 14 knots on 20 tons per day. No longer was the indifferent quality of coal a standing problem even though it was 1953 before the last coal-burner *Port Campbell* (1922) was scrapped. As new building prices stabilized in the mid 1920s seven similar ships to *Port Dunedin* followed.

Ian Farquhar cleverly blends the unfolding economic developments ashore with the Port Line's fleet afloat. At the Ottawa conference of 1932 Britain agreed to buy more food from the

Dominions. Whilst Harland and Wolff developed the 'Empire meat ships' for Shaw Savill and Blue Star, Port Line had Swan Hunter build *Port Jackson* (1937) with refrigeration by cold air as well as abandoning the open forecastle for crew accommodation: ratings were now in two-berth cabins.

For advertising purposes Port Line produced a booklet entitled 'Wartime Experiences' in 1947. With access to Second World War records, Ian Farquhar elaborates on these incidents. There is the story of how *Port Chalmers* (1933), at considerable risk to herself, relayed distress messages from other ships when they were attacked by the raider *Admiral Graf Spee*, thus convincing the Admiralty to position warships and set the scene for the Battle of the River Plate. *Port Chalmers* went on to safely complete two round voyages to assist with the relief of Malta. There is the tale of how the second officer of *Port Brisbane* (1923) might have abandoned her sinking early with he and his boat's crew thus escaping capture by a German raider. Even Ian Farquhar has not been able to find a photo of *Port Jackson's* sister ship *Port Napier* (1940) which, despite vigorous pleas, was requisitioned as a minelayer, and caught fire and blew up in a Scottish sea loch only 11 months later. Another and even more massive explosion was the managed ship *Fort Stikine* (1942) at Bombay in 1944.

It could be said that for many readers the most interesting section of Port Line's history came after the Allied victory in August 1945. Eight days later *Port Lincoln* slid down the ways into the Tyne: what a way to celebrate the end of the war. Planning Port Line's reconstruction and expansion the company had the great good fortune to have a talented duo in Bill Donald and Ronnie Senior - quite outstanding shipping men by any measure.

As a schoolboy commuting on a Sydney Harbour ferry I remember the excitement of seeing *Port Brisbane* heading towards a berth at Prymont on a winter morning in mid 1949. Ten years later as a management trainee in a Liverpool shipping company I had the temerity to enquire of our ships' husband director why couldn't our new buildings be made as attractive? I was told that their trend-setting superstructure was only achieved by number 3 hatch having a 43-foot overhang under it making the hold slow and difficult to stow. Caution forbade me to comment that our flagship *Aureol* had a 52-foot overhang at her number 2 hatch which, as with the Port Line twins, covered the biggest cargo space.

Ian Farquhar charts the progress of Port Line right up to the joint company that became Associated Container Transportation (Aust.) Ltd. (ACTA). On the way we read how growing spending power in Australasia spawned the intermediate-sized ships; the growth of MANZ Line link with North America and the gestation of Crusader; why *Port Hobart* (1946) was the first B&W-engined ship Port Line owned; how other companies' ships displaced from their routes taken up on five year time charters, almost became a fleet-within-a-fleet; the reason why *Port Albany* (1965), *Port Huon* (1965) and *Port Burnie* (1966) were especially built for a one-way Australian fruit export trade that never made money.

Unusually the author labels ships by the year of their build not the more impersonal 1,2,or 3, of the same name. The reproduction of the carefully chosen photos - many of the best from the Bain-Wright Collection - is outstanding. If I have one complaint it is that there are no photos of examples of Port Line's notably stylish accommodation and interiors: space did not allow for it. However, Appendix 5 is made up of 36 paragraphs each a 'Port Line Tale': they add humour and life to this wonderful saga.

Here was a shipping company with a human face that was the source of an outstanding fleet and the services it provided. Ian Farquhar has researched and chronicled Port Line's entire history to near perfection, he can now rest from his labours but many will hope that he will not do so.

Andrew Bell

LIGHT VESSELS OF THE UNITED KINGDOM 1820-2006 ILLUSTRATED FLEET LIST compiled by Philip Simons.
120-page A4 softback published by the WSS Small Craft Group at £14.00.
Light vessels are utterly distinctive, painted red, have a big flashing light, and a name painted in big letters on their hull. Yet for all their recognisability they are somewhat mysterious, as their identities as individual vessels are hard to ascertain. This remarkable publication almost certainly provides the first documentation of British light vessels, and is to be very warmly welcomed. It provides what is

believed to be a complete list of all British light vessels, organised by operating authority: Trinity House, Commissioners of Irish Lights, Northern Lighthouse Board, Humber Conservancy Board, and the Mersey Docks and Harbour Board. For each light vessel is given its number or name, the year and builder, tonnage and dimensions, and what is known about its disposal, including in many cases its present whereabouts. It is profusely illustrated, with general arrangement drawings and photographs, the latter very well reproduced given that short-run printing techniques have clearly been used. Indeed, reproduction can stand comparison with the efforts of publishers who use mainstream printers and appear to have done their scanning on £80 kit from Dixons. There are also lists of light vessel stations round the British Isles and maps. The author admits that this is essentially a fleet list and not a history of the light vessel, and points out that such a history has already been produced by Anthony Lane as 'Guiding Lights'.

The main criticism to be levelled at this book's publishers is that they have been unduly modest. This is a very worthwhile book, well researched and well illustrated. Whilst those producing it have done a more than adequate job, professional typesetting would have enhanced the work as would a little more care in proof reading. Certainly the material they are presenting would fully justify a more ambitious production, perhaps perfect bound with a stiffer cover. Having said that, this reviewer feels no-one who buys the book will be disappointed. It is exactly the sort of work which organisations like the World Ship Society should be producing, books which make available the excellent research their members are undertaking, which will easily recoup their production costs, but are unlikely to be taken up by a 'commercial' publisher.

Roy Fenton

COASTERS OF THE MANCHESTER SHIP CANAL by Bernard McCall.
BRISTOL CHANNEL SHIPPING MEMORIES by Andrew Wiltshire.
Both 80-page hardbacks published by Bernard McCall at £15.00 each.
The hardback landscape picture book has become deservedly popular in recent years, with Priam Publications, Ian Allan and Bernard McCall producing colour pictorials in the format, which lends itself very well to the proportions of the usual transparency of a ship. 'Coasters of the Manchester Ship Canal' makes a virtual journey from the Mersey at Eastham to Manchester Docks, with photographs of coastal vessels either underway or berthed at locations on the way. The captions describe the location, give details of the ship pictured with tonnage, date, usually its builder, a brief description of its history and sometimes its trade, but there is little about its ownership. Photographs have been chosen to show the vessel in its context, which is often industrial. In terms of quality they vary from the highly atmospheric, such as *Sheila Maria* navigating a wintry Weaver, to the frankly rather dull, such as *Stolt Cormorant* in flat summer light at Partington. The criteria for choice has been to show as many locations as possible and whilst this is laudable it means that a number of photographs have been selected which lack impact. This is a choice based on what is available to the publisher and, although this reviewer would go for picture quality every time, the editor's judgement should be respected. Nevertheless, there are plenty of photographs to drool over, in particular some from the cameras of Neil Burns, John Slavin and Ken Lowe.

In contrast, 'Bristol Channel Shipping Memories' has hardly a duff slide in its 80 pages. Depicting ports in the Swansea to Bristol range, the slides are largely the work of the author's father, John Wiltshire, with contributions from Nigel Jones, Derek Chaplin and Bob Allen. Almost all are taken in superb lighting, and even the ships on berths stand out. There are some veterans featured which suggests John Wiltshire devoted much time an effort to photographing interesting ships. Unfortunately, the book is let down by the quality of the captions. Clearly the writer has less feel for the ships than his photographer father. The captions are jerkily written, packed with disjointed facts, and too many contain errors or questionable statements that had this reviewer bristling. Very few meet the criteria of encouraging the reader to look more carefully at the photograph. Buy this book for its superb photographs, not for its captions.

Roy Fenton

INDEX TO RECORD 33 TO 36

Issue numbers are shown in bold

Index of articles

Index of ships

262